Remain on track

Alex Ndukwe

First printing, 2020

Printed in the united states of America

ISBN: 978-1-79486-883-0

Dedication

This book is dedicated to Bishop N.I. Obayojie, General Overseer, Christ Victory Life Church International, a Hero of Faith and a man of God full of wisdom.

Forward

I have been in transition and it has offered me the privilege to reflect on some topical issues in Christendom and the decay that has continued, though it could be attributed to signs of the end time we are to occupy until the day of rapture, most men of God had confirmed that the time is very close.

Love ought to be the greatest but we are very far from this, this should be noticed within our fold before extending it to first-timers and this determines if they will stay or not, follow up and regular visits make new members decide to stay and get encouraged to join the workforce.

The book discusses the personality of Jesus Christ and how we can emulate his behaviours, the benefits to the church and ourselves. The examples are for illustrative purpose and not aimed at castigating or embarrassing anyone.

We are the light of the world but unfortunately, our impact is not felt, darkness still persist in our midst and I want to state that we need to evaluate ourselves and make amends because a filthy heart can be recreated, our hearts must be with Jesus and this will make the work easier.

The book explains all required for us to remain with the almighty and live a holy life, we can achieve a lot in the body of Christ, we must thirst for Christ-like behaviour, it's the only way we can fulfil our mandate as children of God.

We should not just complete the number but make impacts for God either you are a member or a worker, remember that any day to stop making impact shows that you have backslid and that will not be our portion in Jesus name.

Are still warming the seat, please get involved and the reward is enormous, and you will be surprised when you start counting your blessings.

Pastor Alex Ndukwe

Table of content

Remaining on track

I appreciate God Almighty for the grace to put this book project together, with inspiration that I received at Christ Victory Life Church international under the ministration of the presiding Bishop.

Brethren I believe you will imagine what it means to remain on track, don't forget we are pilgrims on earth and running a race and the word of God says in the book of Romans 9 verse 16, 'So then it is not of him that willeth, nor of him that runneth, but of God that sheweth mercy.' We need the help of God in this race we are running for so many reasons, Christianity is not a bed of roses, challenges, trials, temptations must come in various dimensions and only by the mercies of God that we will triumph.

The Christian race is like an athlete running a marathon on the track, should the fellow fall out of the track, the resultant effect is disqualification from the tournament. The works of our hands, behavioural patterns, relationship with God determines how far we can go in this race. I want to refer you to my book titled, 'What's in your heart', explains in details about the spiritual health of our heart and thank God that divided, filthy heart can be recreated, this will definitely help us in this race, the psalmist in psalm 51:10-12, what we need is a new heart and renewal of right spirit within us, a spirit that is not evil rather an excellent one that radiates the virtues of the almighty, this will foster a good relationship with the almighty. God dwells in us and access to secrets. An unsettled heart yields nothing, this fellow cannot enjoy the presence of the holy spirit and the joy of salvation would also be missing. The advice is for such a fellow to thirst for recreation of the heart.

My journey as a programmer and analyst shows that every program cannot be devoid of any subroutine or functions when there is an error it affects the entire solution, the result becomes zero and you have to trace the error, correct it before success can be recorded. This is the same thing in our Christian race. A perfect heart that is not holy is the same as someone that has not experienced salvation. Review of our behaviour is an ongoing process that must be carried out and this will make us better, once we can correct our mistakes, our rating improves.

Brethren we don't have a choice but to ensure we remain on track by ensuring we live holy, have fear of God, ensure our hearts are pure. The holy spirit we help us to finish well in the name of Jesus.

Chapter 1

Whom are you?

This chapter is a question and I want you to ask yourself this question. Do you really know who you are, many in Christendom are operating below per, exercising fear and employing prophets or prophetess that pray for them and give them information concerning their future.

I want to announce to you that the power has already been handed to you, all that is required is to take authority and go ahead to make decrees, declarations. Let me remind you that Luke 10:19(NIV), 'I have given you authority to trample on snakes and scorpions and to overcome all the power of the enemy; nothing will harm you.' God has given us 'authority to trample on snakes and scorpion', what else can be more deadly than these reptiles, even the things that are yet to be invented the Lord has given us power over them, power to subdue every contrary power of the enemy, then why should we nurse fear when we are confronted with challenges, don't forget Isaiah 22:22(KJV), 'And the key of the house of David will I lay upon his shoulder; so he shall open, and none shall shut, and he shall shut, and none shall open.'

Interestingly we will argue that this scripture was a prophecy given by prophet Isaiah before Jesus was born, it applies to us and the proof is found in Romans 8:17, 'And if children, then heirs; heirs of God, and joint-heirs with Christ; if so be that we suffer with him, that we may be also glorified together.' As heir, heir of God and joint-heir with Christ technically means that the Keys of the house of David will be on our shoulder. This makes us dangerous and the capacity to turn things around, any door we shut no man can open and any door we open no man can shut, can you imagine the exploits you can do by yourself.

There is a missing link because most of us lay claims and it cannot be substantiated. ARE YOU APPROVED, how many words of God is in your system, when last did you study the word of God wholeheartedly by meditating and not just reading it like a novel. Obviously, there are different kinds of Children of God i.e. CERTIFIED, FILLER and MIX MULTITUDE.

CERTIFIED - This child of God study's the word of God effectively. 'Study to shew thyself approved unto God, a workman that needeth not to be ashamed, rightly dividing the word of truth.'(2 Timothy 2:15). Heaven has a seal on any word spoken by this child of God and it comes to pass. The enemy has a hold of the scriptures, remember when DEVIL tempted JESUS, you could recall the enemy saying 'It is written....', we must have it on our fingertips, this is the reason why we must be approved. Making decrees and declarations becomes easy because you know which word of God to use and when. Apart from having the word of God handy, this child of God also Trusts God absolutely by exercising Faith. Remains positive no matter the situation that comes his way. Broken, humbled, meek and understands the workings of God.

FILLER – This is a child of God that only attends service but not ready to study the word of God, completes the number in a congregation. The complaints about everything. Claims to trust God but lack faith. His/her Salvation is not genuine, still lives in sin.

MIX MULTITUDE

This child of God is neither here or there, sitting on the fence. Pretends to be a child of God but still lives a life of sin. Some even join the workforce, become a minister and even a pastor. Does not have time to look at the issue from the dimension of a child of God. Argues about the scripture blindly.

Where do you belong? , you can still turn a new leaf, come back to Jesus and become a certified child of God. The classifications we have made is not the ultimate but understand that we need to thirst for perfection, let's look at some examples and I believe it will help all of us and we will not miss the mark in Jesus name. Let us hold and keep the classification at on corner and look at some salient issues.

'Obedience is better than sacrifice', Saul made a mistake by trying to be a priest and King at the same time, this is not possible, we must exercise caution. I want to thank God for the story Bishop obayojie narrated on 12th January 2020 service, I was shocked because I experienced something similar, the Church of God has become a cult and what do we gain by running ourselves down.

A child of God that siphons God's money and moves it to his account and turns around to destroy another person. As a child of God why can't you respect constituted authority, 1 Corinthians 12:5-12, 'And there are differences of administrations, but the same Lord.' And there are diversities of operations, but it is the same God which worketh all in all. But the manifestation of the Spirit is given to every man to profit withal. For to one is given by the Spirit the word of wisdom; to another the word of knowledge by the same Spirit;

To another faith by the same Spirit; to another the gifts of healing by the same Spirit; To another the working of miracles; to another prophecy; to another discerning of spirits; to another divers kinds of tongues; to another the interpretation of tongues: But all these worketh that one and the self-same Spirit, dividing to every man severally as he will. For as the body is one, and hath many members, and all the members of that one body, being many, are one body: so also, is Christ.'

One pitfall is that when we believe we know too much, it becomes difficult to respect leaders put over us, this scripture points out that there is a difference in administration, but they all belong to God. In big churches where pastors are transferred, most workers refer to their former leader and comparing him with the new one and refuse to respect him. Even the small Departments with new Leader, as a worker you must respect them, the ministry is quite different from circular.

I recall some years ago, I was Area Pastor over a parish pastor that was an Asst. Pastor, then I was just a Deacon. This pastor will not respect me and during one of our convections, I distributed levies for 7 parishes for us to hire two buses that would convey our brethren to Redemption camp in Lagos and this pastor refused to contribute when I called him he was already at the camp and I used my money meant for me to buy flight ticket and I used it to complete the payment. Promotion came and I had to nominate a successor, I sent his name and he stepped into my shoes as Area pastor, the pastors under him refused to respect him, refused to contribute money. During our Zonal and Area pastors meeting, his Area had unpaid dues and when the Regional pastor asked him, he said the pastors in his area refused to cooperate, I shook my head because he did the same to me.

Ministry is a different ball game because whatever you sow you must reap and the church I pastored last in FCT the same thing happened, the Sunday school coordinator and the church administrator conspired and ensured they removed me from office, the allegations were baseless. Today he's no longer there, he left by himself, he got the same result, he ensured I was transferred out of this parish and he had issues and was transferred to the main Church and he refused to go and preferred to leave by himself.

Brethren you cannot fight for God, allow the Lord to take charge of every issue, no matter how we think we have been oppressed, vengeance belongs to God, we must take note of this and avoid keeping malice, grudge. This is a poly of the enemy to deprive us of our blessings and inheritance.

Leaders should not abuse their office by doing the wrong thing, the fear of God should be paramount in all our actions, I remember when I manned Gateway Zone, this church became number 2 in RCCG, Region 9, Kano and the Lord helped us so much that we conducted two services on Sundays, our annual thanksgiving service, we had a huge collections and three ministers stormed my office and said I should approve that the collection be split into two and we keep one part and I said NO, we shall remit 100% of the headquarters. As leaders, we need to lead by example. Don't forget Eli and his children, they lost the priesthood because of their excesses, we must be very careful.

As a leader, we must have compassion and behave like a coach, one of my Minister had issues and his ordination letter was seized by the provincial pastor in 2003 and during my time as his pastor in 2008 I decided that he must be ordained, I recommended him that year and before he departed to the Redemption camp I had a session with him, I told him that he must turn a new leaf and stop telling lies if he continues and if he's ordained he will become an anointed lair. He looked sober and promised me he will change, to the glory of God he's now a full pastor and manning a zone.

As a child of God ensure you make an impact in the house of God, the title is not required but with determination, you can excite the almighty, I thank God because my ministry is full of testimonies. Work for God with all your hearts. I want to share this testimony. My house rent was increased from 240K to 350K at Kano in 2009 and I recalled that I had planted 16 parishes, I prayed in my closet and told God to give me my own property in Nasarawa GRA. I engaged the agents and they took me around, the first land was valued =N=15million Naira, I encouraged the agent to look for another property that would be reasonable. The search continued and they took me to another landed property valued at =N=8million Naira. One faithful day I got a phone call from the agent, the story was that there is a house in the GRA that no one wants to buy and it has remained in the market for long and the owner resides at Nguru and needs 4.5million Naira.

We got there and behold it was a Four bedroom bungalow, We called the owner of the property and he confirmed price and I told him I was interested to buy, the process begun, my bank was ready to give me a mortgage facility, we had to conduct a search and discovered it was encumbered, the former owner was a staff of the first bank and the property was not released at Ministry of Land. This was rectified by the Landlord.

I went to my Spiritual Leader, Pastor Akintunde and he encouraged me, spoke a word that nobody will be able to buy this house except I don't show interest. Suddenly people started showing interest and the owner told them except Mr Alex refuses I can't sell to anyone. It took me four months and the owner waited until my bank released a Draft for him and he handed the keys to me. I renovated the house to taste and moved in. I lived in this house until I left kano for Abuja in 2014.

Brethren I'm not boasting, the Lord gave me a house, there is no effort you put into God's business that is a waste. In FCT God helped me also, my parish was paying rent of 6million Naira per annum and this rent was a burden, we started to look for a Land and we saw land for =N=15 million Naira and we negotiated the price to =N=8milliion and we got only =N=5million Naira from our main Church. I had to seek the face of God and the Lord what to do and the Landlady agreed to collect =N=5million Naira as full and final, today the parish has settled there.

From now I want you to realize whom you are in Christ Jesus, 1peter 2:9-10, 'But you are a chosen generation, a royal priesthood, a holy nation, His own special people, that you may proclaim the praises of Him who called you out of darkness into His marvellous light; who once were not a people but are now the people of God, who had not obtained mercy but now have obtained mercy. 'A chosen generation, a royal priesthood, a holy nation', you are very special and it's not by accident, a prince in all respect that carries the power to rattle the kingdom of darkness and a marvellous light that cannot be ignored.

Can you recall the story of Moses when he was picked up by pharaoh's daughter, Exodus 2:5-10,' While Pharaoh's daughter came to the Nile to take a bath, her servants walked along the bank of the river. She saw the basket among the papyrus plants and sent her slave girl to get it. Pharaoh's daughter opened the basket, looked at the baby, and saw it was a boy. He was crying, and she felt sorry for him. She said, "This is one of the Hebrew children." Then the baby's sister asked Pharaoh's daughter, "Should I go and get one of the Hebrew women to nurse the baby for you?" She answered, "Yes!" So the girl brought the baby's mother. Pharaoh's daughter said to the woman, "Take this child, nurse him for me, and I will pay you." She took the child and nursed him. When the child was old enough, she brought him to Pharaoh's daughter, and he became her son. Pharaoh's daughter named him Moses [Pulled Out] and said, "I pulled him out of the water."

Even though Moses lived in the place, his identity as a Hebrew did not change, even as the grandchild of the pharaoh, he had the Hebrew blood and had compassion for his people been maltreated in Egypt. We must know who we are, and the Lord will help us in the name of Jesus.

Chapter 2

Perfect Gift to Mankind

We are called Christians because of Jesus. John 3:16-18, 'For God so loved the world, that he gave his only begotten Son, that whosoever believeth in him should not perish, but have everlasting life. For God sent not his Son into the world to condemn the world; but that the world through him might be saved. He that believeth on him is not condemned: but he that believeth not is condemned already because he hath not believed in the name of the only begotten Son of God.'

No one in our generation can testify to the accuracy of the date of birth of our Lord, Jesus Christ. Jesus was likely not born on 25 December. And this is not disputable! But Christmas is not about the celebration of the "Day" Jesus was born; it has everything to do with the celebration of Jesus Christ - God's Perfect Gift to mankind. The

"Day", 25th December did not die for our sins, to save us from eternal condemnation and reconcile us to God. Jesus did. The "Day", 25th December did not manifest so that it might destroy the works of the devil. Jesus did (1 John 3:8). To celebrate the birth of the Messiah, a "Day" must be set aside in commemoration. And 25th of December happens to be that fortunate Day!

God created man in His own image (Genesis 1:27) and put our pioneer ancestral parents, Adam and Eve in a place of perfect Peace and Treasure (The Garden of Eden) where He only had meetings and direct communications with them, but Adam and Eve disobeyed God and ipso facto lost their right to perfect Peace and Treasure, and in the process, were thrown out of that place of eternal tranquillity by their very Creator, Master and Friend – God. The sin of Adam and Eve rubbed on all generations of mankind. It brought corruption, curse, condemnation and death to the hitherto perfectly and beautifully made creation in God's own image – man and woman.

With sin, "the soul of man experienced a schism with God's Spirit. The only solution to bridge this great divide and bring mankind back in a relationship with God would require a work of atonement." Let me make it abundantly clear here that the work of atonement is not limited to the first sin that Adam and Eve committed, it also takes care of the sins that we ourselves have committed.

Our God is the God of Love (Αγάπη – Agape). His love for man is beyond human imagination and comprehension. To put it more succinctly, He has a ridiculous love for mankind! God knew that man will fall; therefore He provided safeguards for their redemption even before the foundation of the world:

"...but with the precious blood of Christ, as of a lamb without blemish and without spot. He indeed was foreordained before the foundation of the world but was manifest in these last times for you. (I Peter 1:18-20 NKJV).

Jesus is God's perfect Gift (Lamb) that was foreordained for the redemption of man even before the foundation of the world. At the fullness of time, He came into the earth that He made through the birth process. He wrapped Himself in flesh and blood and chose to be born of a woman like every human being, to fulfil that purpose: But when the fullness of the time had come, God sent forth His Son, born of a woman, born under the law, to redeem those who were under the law, that we might receive the adoption as sons. And because you are sons, God has sent forth the Spirit of His Son into your hearts, crying out, "Abba, Father!" Therefore, you are no longer a slave but a son, and if a son, then an heir of God through Christ. (Galatians 4:4-7 NKJV).

Realising the gravity of the yoke of the burden of the law under which we were condemned because of sin, which Jesus' ultimate sacrifice broke, no celebration to commemorate

Him on the date of His birth is enough! When the Apostle Paul wrote that God sent Jesus in order to redeem those under the law, he was talking about all generations of mankind – you and me. We were lost in our sins and separated from God. We could not on our own restore ourselves to a relationship with Him, but God wanted us to be free to re-establish a relationship with Him. In order to remove the barrier that stood in-between our relationship with Him, God sent Jesus "that we might receive the adoption as [His] sons and daughters if you like.

The announcement of the birth of Messiah, Luke 1:26-38(GNT), 'In the sixth month of Elizabeth's pregnancy God sent the angel Gabriel to a town in Galilee named Nazareth. He had a message for a young woman promised in marriage to a man named Joseph, who was a descendant of King David. Her name was Mary. The angel came to her and said, "Peace be with you! The Lord is with you and has greatly blessed you!" Mary was deeply troubled by the angel's message, and she wondered what his words meant. The angel said to her, "Don't be afraid, Mary; God has been gracious to you. You will become pregnant and give birth to a son, and you will name him Jesus. He will be great and will be called the Son of the Highest God. The Lord God will make him a king, as his ancestor David was, and he will be the king of the descendants of Jacob forever; his kingdom will never end!" Mary said to the angel, "I am a virgin. How, then, can this be?" The angel answered, "The Holy Spirit will come on you, and God's power will rest upon you. For this reason, the holy child will be called the Son of God.

Remember your relative Elizabeth. It is said that she cannot have children, but she herself is now six months pregnant, even though she is very old. For there is nothing that God cannot do." "I am the Lord's servant," said Mary; "may it happen to me as you have said." And the angel left her.

The birth of Jesus was extraordinary in the sense that Mary conceived without meeting a man, Mary informed the angel but I'm a virgin how will it be and the angel explained how the holy ghost will come upon her and conception would take place, this is wonderful, mysteries that defiled logic of human comprehension and genetic science. This not only proofs how powerful God is but the DNA of Jesus is that of the Almighty God. The statement that 'Jesus Christ' is the son of God is a fact and not fiction. The second Adam sent to the world to wipe off the iniquities of the first Adam and ensuring a better relationship with God, an end to sacrifice of bulls, lambs etc, an end to the holies of holies, Man could gain direct access to our creator, man could enjoy salvation free of charge.

Let us look at the prophecy given by prophet Isaiah before the birth of Jesus, Isaiah 9:6(GNT), 'A child is born to us! A son is given to us! And he will be our ruler. He will be called, "Wonderful[a] Counsellor," "Mighty God," "Eternal Father,"

"Prince of Peace." We are going to interpret the names ascribed to Jesus in this scripture.

Wonderful Counsellor

That Isaiah calls the Messiah the "Wonderful Counsellor" indicates the kind of character this coming King has. The word wonderful in this passage literally means "incomprehensible." The Messiah will cause us to be "full of wonder." The word is much weightier than the way it's used in normal conversation today—we say things are "wonderful" if they are pleasant, lovely, or the least bit likeable. Jesus is wonderful in a way that is boggling to the mind. The same word for "wonderful" is used in Judges 13:18 when Manoah, Samson's father, asked the LORD (in a theophany) what His name was. The angel of the LORD responded, "Why do you ask my name, seeing it is wonderful?" In other words, "Why do you ask my name, since it is beyond your understanding?"

Jesus demonstrated His wonderfulness in various ways when He was on the earth, beginning with His conception in the womb of a virgin (Matthew 1:23). He showed He is the "wonderful" One in His power to heal (Matthew 4:23), His amazing teaching (Mark 1:22), His perfect life (Hebrews 4:15), and His resurrection from the dead (Mark 16:6). Jesus taught many wonderful things that are counterintuitive to the human mind: "Blessed are those who mourn" (Matthew 5:4). "Rejoice and be glad" in persecution (Matthew 5:11–12). "Love your enemies, do good to those who hate you" (Luke 6:27). Jesus' kind of wonderful is awe-inspiring and superior to any other kind, for He is perfect in every way (Matthew 5:48).

The second part of the Messiah's title is the word counsellor. In ancient Israel, a counsellor was portrayed as a wise king, such as Solomon, giving guidance to his people (1 Kings 4:34; Micah 4:9). Isaiah uses this word again in 28:29 to describe the LORD: "This also comes from the LORD of hosts; he is wonderful in counsel and excellent in wisdom." Jesus is a wise counsellor. "He did not need any testimony about mankind, for he knew what was in each person" (John 2:25). He is able to advise His people thoroughly because He is qualified in ways no human counsellor is. In Christ is "hidden all the treasures of wisdom and knowledge" (Colossians 2:3), including the knowledge of all human nature (Psalm 139:1–2). Jesus always knows what we are going through, and He always knows the right course of action (Hebrews 4:15–16).

Christ's position as our Wonderful Counsellor means we can trust Him to listen to our problems and guide us in the right direction (Proverbs 3:6). We can be sure He is listening because He told us to pray to Him about our worries (Philippians 4:6; James 1:5). We can be certain He has our best interests at heart because He loves us (1 John 4:19). And His love is so wide and deep (and wonderful) that we cannot fully understand it (Romans 5:8).

Mighty God

This name is the compound Hebrew title El Gibbor, and both parts of the name need to be understood "God." The first part of the title is El, the singular form of the word Elohim. In the Old Testament, this referred to the one true God (though on occasion it was used of mighty heroes or even false gods). Yet even though Jesus Himself pointed out that the title is sometimes used of mighty sons of men (JN. 10:34), the title is so often used of God and only God, that the prophet Hosea used El to set God in contrast to the man in Hosea 11:9. That Isaiah 9:6 was predicted- in One who would be far more than a man is indicated by the third name "Everlasting Father" and by the New Testament record of Christ. The Christ who walked on water died voluntarily for our sins, and then physically rose from the dead is the One who also said, "Before Abraham was, I am" (JN. 8:58). He is the One of whom John wrote:

In the beginning, was the Word, and the Word was with God, and the Word was God. He was at the beginning with God. All things were made through Him, and without Him, nothing was made that was made (JN. 1:1-3).

"Mighty." The other part of the name is Gibbor, which means "strength, power, hero." What a statement! In a world where heroes are often determined by athletic prowess, personal talent, or financial power, we are told that the only One truly worthy to be called "hero" is the One whose might is unparalleled. The focus of Isaiah's prophecy is El Gibbor, the mighty God who is our true Hero. What this prophet in the seventh century BC anticipated, the New Testament confirms. Because the Messiah would be God, He would have God's power—but to Isaiah, the amazing thing was that the Messiah would not only have the power of God, He would be the God of power!

What is the evidence that Jesus Christ is the "Mighty God"?

His perfect life, sacrificial death, and resurrection, He showed we could trust Him, though most of His own people rejected Him. John wrote, "He came to His own, and His own did not receive Him" (JN. 1:11). Yet in many cases, He was recognized as the long-awaited Messiah. Nicodemus, a rabbi of Israel, recognized Him (cp. JN. 3 with JN.19). The disciples recognized Him (compare MT. 8:27 with 16:16). Mary Magdalene recognized Him, and her life was transformed (LK. 8:2). Others' lives were changed as well, including the church's most feared persecutor, Saul of Tarsus (ACTS 9).

These and thousands of other first-century people believed—and for good reason. Jesus Christ proved Himself to be El Gibbor as He displayed His life-changing might and power. Still today, for those who see their need of a Saviour, the evidence of Christ's mighty power is overwhelming. For those who sense their own inability to live up to God's standard, the apostle

John wrote, "As many as received Him, to them He gave the right to become children of God, to those who believe in His name" (JN. 1:12).

The New Testament provides us with an opportunity to see the fullness of the "Mighty God" Isaiah predicted, showing both how His power was displayed in His life on earth—but also how it was seen before He even came to the earth.

Jesus showed His right to be recognized as the Mighty God by demonstrating power over nature (LK. 5:1-11), power over disease (MT. 9:18-26), power over demons (LK. 8:26-39), power over sin (MK. 2:3-12), and power over death (1 COR. 15:1-19). Throughout the course of His public life, Christ revealed His divine might in ways that not only were undeniable (ACTS 2:22) but also intentional validations of His claim to be God (JN. 20:30-31). When we see the otherwise inexplicable demonstrations of God's might in the unparalleled life of Christ, it becomes clear why Paul would call Jesus "the Son of God with power" (ROM. 1:4) and

"Christ the power of God and the wisdom of God"
(1 COR. 1:24).

What is the importance of the name
"Mighty God" to believers today? While
appreciating the evidence that shows Christ to be
the Mighty God, we must remember that this is
more than mere theological data. It is inspired
evidence that urges us to see and respond to
Christ as He is—our "Mighty God." He is the source
of our power In Acts 1:8, Jesus promised to send
the power of the Holy Spirit to enable us to be His
representatives in the world. Inherent to this
provision of the Spirit is the fact that He wants us to
live distinctive lives in an impure world as evidence
of His presence in us.

He is the strength of our lives. In Philippians
4:13, Paul wrote, "I can do all things through Christ
who strengthens me." What a great promise! He
will strengthen us for all the circumstances and
inevitabilities of life. This doesn't mean that we will
never know pain or hardship, but that we can

endure in triumph. How can we do that? Only as we rest in His power, not in our own.

He secures our eternity. The apostle Peter wrote that we are "kept by the power of God" (1 PET. 1:5). Nothing can overcome God's power to keep us in Christ. What a great assurance it is to know that we are secure not because of our own ability to hold on to Him, but by His power holding on to us. In view of the evidence, how can we see our Lord Jesus Christ as anything less than the Mighty God, El Gibbor? In 1885, J. B. Figgis took it even further, describing in his book Emmanuel the surprising way in which the Mighty God not only showed His might by miracles, but also by His disarming meekness:

Christ's inimitable meekness and patience never once forsook Him in a vexatious, ungrateful, cruel sphere. He never stepped out of the humble sphere in which He was brought up; He does not seem to have ever possessed for Himself so much as the smallest coin, and when He died had no means for providing for His mother, and could only commend her to one of His disciples. Yet, His life was infinitely superior to all others. If Jesus were no more than a man or a hero, why are there not more men like Him? What God did for one man, God would certainly do for others. It is unaccountable that it has never been done. The incarnation, when Jesus came as "the Mighty God," alone helps us to the solution of such an enigma.

Eternal Father

Without the assurance of His care, I look to other people and things to satisfy my deepest heart longings, but by relying on the Eternal Father I can trust Him to always lovingly care and watch over my life needs. The Lord is Eternal Father! We are not content to only own great counsel. The man also needs the warmth of God's love. This love and security of God is the cornerstone of our lives.

Modern psychology seems to think they have fully identified the basic need of a man in his need for self-esteem. Along this same line, we hear many Christians are saying that we need to love ourselves more so that we can love others. This is not Christ's command.

If man lives the secular life excluding God from his life, his solutions will always focus on what he sees. We are not saying that love from one's parents is not important. They are crucial for a healthy start in life. Many of our insecurities and diseases come from not being properly cared for while young. But our solutions are not found there. Our lives need to centre around our Eternal Father. God's sacrifice of His one Son enabled many to be His sons. Listen to the simple words of John issuing forth some of the most wonderful words we could here. These words from our very adoption papers.

"But as many, as received Him, to them He gave the right to become children of God, even to those who believe in His name, who were born not of blood, nor of the will of the flesh, nor of the will of man, but of God" (John 1:12).

Some think God is our natural Father because man is made in the image of God. No, no Jesus said. Jesus said our natural father is the devil. He simply told them it is easy to identify the father by what the child does. It is the principle of imitation. God was gracious; we are to be forgiving. God is faithful; we need to be faithful. God is truthful; we need to be truthful. If you find a contradiction, you need to start wondering about your life or your relationship. Something is wrong.

Prince of Peace

In a world filled with war and violence, it's difficult to see how Jesus could be the all-powerful God who acts in human history and be the embodiment of peace. But physical safety and political harmony don't necessarily reflect the kind of peace He's talking about (John 14:27).

The Hebrew word for "peace," shalom, is often used in reference to an appearance of calm and tranquillity of individuals, groups, and nations. The Greek word eirene means "unity and accord"; Paul uses eirene to describe the objective of the New Testament church. But the deeper, more foundational meaning of peace is "the spiritual harmony brought about by an individual's restoration with God."

In our sinful state, we are enemies with God (Romans 5:10). "But God demonstrates His own love toward us, in that while we were yet sinners, Christ died for us" (Romans 5:8). Because of Christ's sacrifice, we are restored to a relationship of peace with God (Romans 5:1). This is the deep, abiding peace between our hearts and our Creator that cannot be taken away (John 10:27–28) and the ultimate fulfilment of Christ's work as "Prince of Peace."

But Christ's sacrifice provides more for us than eternal peace; it also allows us to have a relationship with the Holy Spirit, the Helper who promises to guide us (John 16:7, 13). Further, the Holy Spirit will manifest Himself in us by having us live in ways we couldn't possibly live on our own, including filling our lives with love, joy, and peace (Galatians 5:22–23). This love, joy, and peace are all results of the Holy Spirit working in the life of a believer. They are reflections of His presence in us. And, although their deepest, most vital result is to have us live in love, joy, and peace with God, they can't help but spill over into our relationships with people.

And we desperately need it—especially since God calls us to live with singleness of purpose with other believers, with humility, gentleness, and patience, "being diligent to preserve the unity of the Spirit in the bond of peace" (Ephesians 4:1–3). This unity in purpose and gentleness would be impossible without the work of the Holy Spirit in us and the peace we have with God thanks to the sacrifice of His Son.

Ironically, the lightest definition of peace, that of the appearance of tranquillity in a person, can be the most difficult to grasp and maintain.

Remain on Track

We do nothing to acquire or maintain our spiritual peace with God (Ephesians 2:8–9). And, while living in unity with other believers can be extremely difficult, living in peace in our own lives can very often feel impossible. Note that peaceful doesn't mean "easy." Jesus never promised easy; He only promised help. In fact, He told us to expect tribulation (John 16:33) and trials (James 1:2). But He also said that, if we called on Him, He would give us the "peace of God, which surpasses all comprehension" (Philippians 4:6–7). No matter what hardships we are faced with, we can ask for a peace that comes from the powerful love of God that is not dependent on our own strength or the situation around us.

Chapter 3

Christ-like Behaviour

Every Child of God has to emulate the behaviour of Jesus but unfortunately, most of us are far from the mark, I recall a minister in one of our churches made this statement, 'I don't transact business with born again Christians, most times it will end up at the police station, rather I prefer dealing with unbelievers', the day I heard this, I was shocked and I looked at the mouth of that fellow.

My bible tells me in 2 Corinthians 6:14, 'Do not be unequally yoked with unbelievers. For what partnership can righteousness have with wickedness? Or what fellowship does light have with darkness?' unfortunately this statement made in the first paragraph is unfortunate and an embarrassment in Christendom, what has light got to do with darkness?

The enemy has entered the church and we must be conscious of this but if the fire is burning earnestly in our churches, impurities will be burnt, and the environment becomes very pure. On the spot assessment, most of us that are Christians, church workers, Pastors do not exhibit Christ-like behaviour, and this is responsible for our inability to take our rightful position in the society. Our inability to settle scores on our knees, this is because we are pretending and not pure in hearts.

Thank God for the motto of Christ victory Life Church which is 'Love is the greatest', God is Love and it is because of his love for us that he sent his only begotten son to this world to die for our sins. Jesus in his earthly ministry exhibited love beyond measure.

Some General Overseers you cannot see them in their office, it's tug of war, can you imagine blind Bartimaeus calling the attention of a General overseer, what is likely to happen is that he will be carried out and denied access, Jesus showed compassion when he had the call, he simply asked, What can I do for you? And the conversation began, and he received his healing. The story of the woman in Mathew 15:25 -27, 'The woman came and knelt before Him. "Lord, help me!" she said. But Jesus replied, "It is not right to take the children's bread and toss it to the dogs." "Yes, Lord," she said, "even the dogs eat the crumbs that fall from their master's table." ...

Jesus full of compassion, even an unbeliever got attention and responded in verse 28, '"O woman," Jesus answered, "your faith is great! Let it be done for you as you desire." And her daughter was healed from that very hour.'

How do you treat unbelievers? we need to show them, love, leave an impact that will always ring in their hearts and someday they will want to experience salvation to emulate you. Please don't Jude them, love them and bring them to Christ.

Among ourselves do we really exhibit Love? , often we lay claims about this and there is no proof to substantiate this claim. 1 John 4:20, 'If a man says, I love God, and hateth his brother, he is a liar: for he that loveth not his brother whom he hath seen, how can he love God whom he hath not seen?' , If we can exhibit Love and it radiates in our heart, this implies that we are bound to love ourselves and love God the more, it this happens pastors would not need to struggle, everyone will fall in line.

Evangelism will be done at ease without struggling, I had another comment from another minister, 'There is no need to invite too many people, let us remain the way we are', I consider this statement from the pit of hell, then what legacy are we trying to leave behind if we cannot witness and win souls. It should not be a burden but a very important assignment in the vineyard. How can we show the unsaved what we enjoy and depopulate the Kingdom of darkness?

Have you ever imagined what happens when there is a power failure, darkness engulfs the whole environment, you cannot move and suddenly power is restored, darkness is absorbed, and Joy fills the air. This description fits us as light to the world, our duty is to fill the whole place with Joy, cause the downcast to be happy, the sorrowful have reasons to wear a good smile. This is our calling as children of God.

As the Light of the world, anywhere we find ourselves our standard remains to make positive impacts upon lives by dispelling every darkness, the man at the pool of Bethesda with infirmities for 38 years(John 5:8) and when Jesus stepped in, Jesus asked him will you be made whole and the sick man came with excuses that there's no one to help carry him to the pool when there is turbulence in the pool but he didn't know that help had come, Jesus made pronouncement, 'Rise up and walk' and instantly he was made whole.

What of Simon Peter and his friend in Luke 5:1-7, they had toiled all day they couldn't catch a single fish, Jesus had just finished using one of their boats for evangelism, he instructed that they launch into the deep for a drought, Simon spoke with his own wisdom, 'we have toiled all night and could not catch any fish', reluctantly he carried out the instruction and the story was different, bible recorded that they caught all manner of fishes and their net broke, they had to beckon unto their friends to support them in carrying the fishes caught. Simeon broke down after the incidence and said that his sins were much and that Jesus should forgive him, Jesus said soon he will become fishers of men.

These two paragraphs show that Jesus was full of compassion and everywhere he went, he did good and proved that he was indeed light. When last did you have compassion for people? I am asking you this simple question, can people see you like light and in your neighbourhood how do people see you? , there is a thin line between been a custodian of the word of God and been a doer of the word. I have seen lots of wickedness among brethren and you will imagine if some of us ever experienced salvation.

I will tell you a story, there is no need to mention names, a General Overseer of a church-based in port Harcourt wrote a petition against a brother in my parish that happens to be a Sunday school teacher when this brother handles a Sunday school session you will discover he has strong knowledge of the scripture considering the manner in which he links the scriptures.

One faithful afternoon I had to see my Regional pastor, he asked me whether I know the brother and I confirmed that he is the coordinator of Sunday school in my parish and daddy then informed me that someone wrote a petition against him and behold I was instructed that me and another senior pastor should preside over the matter and settle the parties involved.

We made the first attempt and the man of God didn't show up, we had to adjourn the deliberation, this time my beloved brother reported the matter to EFCC and unfortunately, the senior pastor had travelled to the United States for vacation, another petition was written and

Daddy gives me the power to resolve the issue since the other pastor was out of the country. I called my brother and informed him that we must settle the dispute between him and General overseer.

Brethren please don't be bored with this illustration it will be us, the first thing I did was to pray and ask God for guidance, the holy spirit instructed me to invite one Deacon in the main church, he happens to be the overall coordinator for Sunday school. I called him and told him that he will have to attend the session and he obliged. I had to call the General Overseer and he gave me his convenient date and the meeting was fixed and notices circulated to all parties involved.

We had the meeting at my office in the parish, I had to invite my accountant that happens to be elderly, I prayed before we commenced deliberations. I made a brief comment and declared that the holy ghost will help us and the parties should feel free. I asked my brother to tell us what happened, he said that the General overseer is owing to him 5 Million Naira and he must pay him, no going back. Interestingly the Deacon raised his hand and said, 'Pastor I was part of this transaction, I travelled with him to NDDC and with my background as an Auditor I advised him to be careful and avoid incurring a loss', I was shocked because I didn't know why the holy ghost insisted that I should involve him and he went further to inform us that my beloved brother gave someone a bribe of =N=3million Naira and the fellow was supposed to take him to the Managing Director of NDDC and he vanished with the money and he was introduced by the General Overseer who happens to be an engineer at NDDC.

I asked the General overseer to make his own comments based on what we have heard, he said truly the man that received =N=3million was introduced by him and there was another 1.5 Million Naira given to him and he had already paid the money to EFCC. This led to a deadlock in our deliberations, I had to bend down my head and prayed, the holy spirit instructed that I should tell my beloved brother to write off the =N=3.5 million he was claiming and good business will come in the future.

My beloved brother refused, and the deacon made another contribution and asked him to listen to my advice and that's the only way we can resolve the matter and he then agreed. The General overseer was glad, and he thanked me and I said to him let us thank God.

Brethren these are Christians, my beloved brother forgot that with God nothing shall be impossible(Luke 1:37), he made a mistake by not trusting God, giving that bribe was not necessary, the flesh was in control and not the spirit, we shouldn't have gotten to this point in the first place, the General Overseer should have been more careful with issues like this, he wrote a petition when he should have seen the face of God. My beloved brother happens to be very transactional, should have had compassion and listen to his pastor, the spirit of pride was in control.

My beloved brother nursed a grudge against me because of this Judgement that was passed. I appreciate God because I ensure I always seek his face before taking any decision, Forgiveness is the bedrock of our beliefs as Christians but most of us would rather take vengeance and we need to watch this and pray that God helps us to overcome this spirit of vengeance.

These are Christians and the incidence is regarded as a shame to the body of Christ and we must ensure we turn a new leaf and be an epistle for men to read, 2 Corinthians 3:2, 'Ye are our epistle written in our hearts, known and read of all men:' it is not impossible for comments like, 'If my beloved brother is a Christian then I'm pope', an unbeliever would definitely make such assertions to make mockery of our faith and we must guard against it. They are watching and our behavioural pattern can be an epistle written in their hearts that is bound to bring them to Christ without anyone preaching to them.

Remain on Track

We appreciate God for the illustration above and let us look at some traits of our Lord Jesus Christ that we must emulate, they are as follows:

- Compassionate

- Servant

- Loving

- Forgiving

- Committed

- Prayerful

- Gentleness

- Self-Control

- Patience

- Humble

1) **Compassionate**

Jesus never looked away from people; He always looked upon them and had compassion (Matthew 9:36). Whenever people were around him, Jesus understood what their real needs were and sought to address them. For some, physical healing was necessary, for others the root issue was spiritual. In all cases though, Jesus took the time to notice that people were hurting—and His compassion drove Him to help them.

2) **Servant**

Without a doubt, Jesus was the ultimate servant. Although He was praised as a great teacher and even had a decent following, He made sure to teach them to be servants by doing it himself. In Mark 10:45, Jesus even tells everyone: "the Son of Man came not to be served but to serve" Despite having the authority to get anything He wanted, have people praise and pamper him, He did the exact opposite by lowering himself and serving others. How many of us are servants? It is very difficult to see such traits in us today, Our Leaders find it difficult to make themselves available, you must book an appointment like people in the world to see them for help and necessary counselling. The crux of the matter is that pride has taken a greater part of us. Pastors employ services of a bodyguard, Psalm 91:1-12 says 'For He will command His angels concerning you to guard you in all your ways. They will lift you up in their hands so that you will not strike your foot against a stone....', this scripture indicates that you must rely on the almighty for protection.

Accordingly, he was prophesied to be the Servant of the Lord (Zechariah 3:8; Isaiah 42:1). In the fullness of time he was sent and came not to be ministered to, as a monarch, but to minister as a servant under the law. His infancy in Egypt, where the Israelites were enslaved, was an emblem of that servile state he was come into, and very early he declared that he must be about his Father's business.

As a servant, he had much work to do, and that very laborious. This was not only in working miracles, which were works his Father gave him to finish, as demonstrations of his Deity; nor only in going about from place to place to heal all manner of diseases, and so doing good to the bodies of men; nor only in preaching the gospel, for which he was qualified and sent, and thereby did good to the souls of men; but chiefly in fulfilling the law of God in the stead of his people.

But his greatest service was the redemption and salvation of men; for this was the work assigned to him by God his Father "to raise up the tribes of Jacob, and to restore the preserved of Israel." This was the work which was before him when became, and this is the work he has finished, for he has obtained eternal redemption and has become the author of eternal salvation.

Now, throughout the whole of his work as a servant, he appeared very diligent and constant. Very early he discovered an eager inclination to be about it, and he was continually, constantly employed in it (John 4:34; 9:4). Nor did he stop working till he had completed the whole. In all which he was faithful to God who appointed him, which is why he justly obtained the character of God's "righteous Servant" (Isaiah 11:5; 53:11). The nine characteristics of Jesus as a servant that we must follow:

1)   Isaiah Describes the Messiah (Jesus) as a Servant

The Old Testament prophet Isaiah speaks of the coming "Messiah" as a servant. In his writing, the prophet points out the characteristics of a servant-leader. Isaiah wrote,

"Here is my servant, whom I uphold, my chosen one in whom I delight; I will put my Spirit on him, and he will bring justice to the nations. He will not shout or cry out, or raise his voice in the streets. A bruised reed he will not break, and a smouldering wick he will not snuff out. In faithfulness, he will bring forth justice;

he will not falter or be discouraged till he establishes justice on earth. In his teaching, the islands will put their hope." (Isaiah 42:1-4, NIV)

In these words, the prophet is pointing out the unique characteristics of a servant-leader.

2) Jesus Describes Himself as a Servant in His Teaching

In three of the Gospels, Jesus refers to himself and his ministry in the world. Also, in these three passages of scripture, Christ lays out the characteristics of real servanthood. " For even the Son of Man did not come to be served, but to serve, and to give his life as a ransom for many." – Mark 10:45 (NIV)

"...I have come down from heaven not to do my will but to do the will of him who sent me. – John 6:38 (NIV)

"For who is greater, the one who is at the table or the one who serves? Is it not the one who is at the table? But I am among you as one who serves." – Luke 22:27 (NIV)

Jesus points out in these three scriptures some truths about servanthood. He teaches that a real servant leader:

- does not seek service for themselves
- aims to serve others
- does not propose to do his own will
- does not promote himself

Jesus Shows Himself as a Servant By His Actions One of the strongest examples of the servant attitude of Jesus is when he washes his disciples' feet in John, chapter 13.

It was just before the Passover Festival. Jesus knew that the hour had come for him to leave this world and go to the Father. Having loved his own who were in the world, he loved them to the end. The evening meal was in progress, and the devil had already prompted Judas, the son of Simon Iscariot, to betray Jesus. Jesus knew that the Father had put all things under his power and that he had come from God and was returning to God; so he got up from the meal, took off his outer clothing, and wrapped a towel around his waist. After that, he poured water into a basin and began to wash his disciples' feet, drying them with the towel that was wrapped around him. He came to Simon Peter, who said to him, "Lord, are you going to wash my feet?" Jesus replied, "You do not realize now what I am doing, but later you will understand." "No," said Peter, "you shall never wash my feet." Jesus answered, "Unless I wash you, you have no part with me." "Then, Lord," Simon Peter replied, "not just my feet but my hands and my head as well!" Jesus answered, "Those who have had a bath need only to wash their feet; their whole body is clean. And you are clean, though not every one of you." For he knew who was going to betray him, and that was why he said not every one was clean. When he had finished washing their feet, he put on his clothes and returned to his place. "Do you understand what I have done for you?" he asked them. "You call me 'Teacher' and 'Lord,' and rightly so, for that is what I am. Now that I, your Lord and Teacher, have washed your feet, you also should wash one another's feet. I have set you an example that you should do as I have done for you. Very truly I tell you, no servant is greater than his master, nor is a messenger greater than the one who sent him. Now that you know these things, you will be blessed if you do them.

Many people do not readily accept the idea of becoming a servant.

Simon Peter had a difficult time allowing Jesus to wash his feet. This action was the role of the "servant." Jesus made it clear to Simon that this was foundational for all that he had taught the disciples.

4) The Apostle Paul describes Jesus as a Servant

In his letter to the first-century church at Philippi, the Apostle Paul had this to say about the servant role of Jesus,

"Who, being in very nature God, did not consider equality with God something to be used to his own advantage; rather, he made himself nothing by taking the very nature of a servant, being made in human likeness." – Philippians 2:6-7 (NIV) "

Paul also taught the early Christian believers that servanthood and humility work together. He wrote about the example that Jesus set.

"And being found in appearance as a man, he humbled himself by becoming obedient to death—even death on a cross!" – Philippians 2:8 (NIV)

Therefore, Paul points out to the believers that Christ's example of servanthood is one of the most influential messages of the New Testament church.

5) Jesus Was Not a Self-Promoting Servant

Jesus had several opportunities to promote himself. He never did. The Gospel of Matthew tells a story of how Jesus had every opportunity to promote himself but refused to do it. One of those stories can be seen here in the Gospel of Matthew.

Departing from there, He went into their synagogue. And a man was there whose hand was withered. And they questioned Jesus, asking, "Is it lawful to heal on the Sabbath?"—so that they might accuse Him. And He said to them, "What man is there among you who has a sheep, and if it falls into a pit on the Sabbath, will he not take hold of it and lift it out? How much more valuable then is a man than a sheep! So then, it is lawful to do good on the Sabbath." Then He *said to the man, "Stretch out your hand!" He stretched it out, and it was restored to normal, like the other. But the Pharisees went out and conspired against Him, as to how they might destroy Him. But Jesus, aware of this, withdrew from there. Many followed

Him, and He healed them all and warned them not to tell who He was. This was to fulfil what was spoken through Isaiah the prophet: "Behold, My Servant whom I have chosen; My Beloved in whom My soul is well-pleased; I will put My Spirit upon Him, And He shall proclaim justice to the Gentiles. "He will not quarrel, nor cry out; Nor will anyone hear His voice in the streets. "A battered reed He will not break off, And a smouldering wick He will not put out Until He leads justice to victory. "And in His name, the Gentiles will hope." – Matthew 12:9-21

6) Jesus Taught His Disciples That Greatness is Found in Servanthood

"Jesus called them together and said, "You know that the rulers of the Gentiles lord it over them, and their high officials exercise authority over them. Not so with you. Instead, whoever wants to become great among you must be your servant, and whoever wants to be first must be your slave just as the Son of Man did not come to be served, but to serve, and to give his life as a ransom for many." -Matthew 20:25-28 (NIV)

7) Jesus as a Servant Leader, Taught That Humility and Servanthood Cannot be Separated

Christ said to His disciples in the Gospel of Matthew.

"But when you give to the needy, do not let your left hand know what your right hand is doing, so that your giving may be in secret. Then your Father, who sees what is done in secret, will reward you." – Matthew 6:3-4 (NIV)

8) Jesus Praises the Character of a Trusting Servant

Real and powerful servanthood starts by recognizing the power of others. A centurion soldier came to Jesus asking for help. Matthew records the story.

When Jesus had entered Capernaum, a centurion came to him, asking for help. "Lord," he said, "my servant lies at home paralyzed, suffering terribly." Jesus said to him, "Shall I come and heal him?" The centurion replied, "Lord, I do not deserve to have you come under my roof. But just say the word, and my servant will be healed. For I myself am a man under authority, with soldiers under me. I tell this one, 'Go,' and he goes; and that one, 'Come,' and he comes. I say to my servant, 'Do this,' and he does it." When Jesus heard this, he was amazed and said to those following him, "Truly I tell you, I have not found anyone in Israel with such great faith." – Matthew 8:5-10

This story has a significant meaning. Here is a soldier who has authority and power at his fingertips. Yet, he placed himself under the authority of Jesus. The encounter with this soldier impressed Jesus. The man was willing to place himself under the authority and leadership of Jesus much like a servant. This centurion is a perfect example of humble servanthood. As a result, Jesus said, "Truly I tell you, I have not found anyone in Israel with such great faith."

Jesus as a Servant Leader is a Powerful Example to Follow

When thinking about the servant style of Jesus, it would benefit any leader to follow his example. John Stott put it this way, "The authority by which the Christian leader leads is not power but love, not force but example, not coercion but reasoned persuasion. Leaders have power, but power is safe only in the hands of those who humble themselves to serve."

3) **Loving**

Obviously, Jesus had a love for others. If He didn't, He wouldn't be compassionate nor a servant. Jesus claimed that there is no greater love than to die for one of your friends—and He did just that. If anyone doubts His love, all they must do is look upon the cross and see the agony that He bore for their sakes. He experienced that horrible death so that all can be saved. That, very clearly, is true love at its finest. This ingredient is missing in our fold today and this is the reason why some churches will not grow; many have stopped attending their towns meeting and the church must love them when they cannot notice it they leave. Though we need to thank God for some ministries considering the way they show love and we must continue to keep it up and never drop the standards set, it should get better.

4) **Forgiving**

One of the most startling things said in Scripture is found in Luke 23:34, when Jesus is on the cross and proclaims: "Father, forgive them, for they know not what they do." Even while bleeding and experiencing pain, Jesus had His heart set on forgiveness—even forgiving those who put Him there in the first place! This is contrary to the everyday mantra of looking out for number one and obtaining personal justice. Jesus was by no means concerned for His own life; all He wanted was to provide a way for forgiveness. We need to ensure that this trait is part of us, no matter what anyone has done to us, please let us forgive and when we refuse it becomes difficult for our prayers to be answered, we create a hindrance. When you cannot forgive what can of prayer do you want to offer, wasted efforts that cannot yield results. I hear some parents refusing to forgive their children, spouse etc. , this should stop and we should understand that this institution is very important to our society and if cannot be in peace then there is an issue. Forgiveness is key, Romans 12:18-19, 'If it is possible on your part, live at peace with everyone. Do not avenge yourselves, beloved, but leave room for God's wrath. For it is written: "Vengeance is Mine; I will repay, says the Lord." ...

For Jesus, forgiveness is of paramount importance. It is the flip side of the love coin. Love ranks first, the top side, heads. Jesus wants us to love one another as he has loved us, and he explained that the way that people will know that we are his disciples is by the love that we have for one another (Jn 15:12,15; 13:35). But our love is imperfect. We damage our relationship with God and neighbour when we sin, the coin flips, tails. To remain in sin and alienation is to be in a tailspin. Forgiveness is the way to turn the coin back to heads and return to love.

Jesus often spoke about forgiveness, forgave those who sinned against others, forgave those who sinned against him and asked the Church to continue his healing ministry. Jesus taught, "If you forgive others their transgressions, your heavenly Father will forgive you" (Mt 6:14). Peter asked Jesus how often it is necessary to forgive, and Jesus replied, "Seventy-seven times" (Mt 18:22), a number to be taken symbolically, not literally, for the never-ending way that we ought to forgive.

Jesus liked to use parables to illustrate various aspects of forgiveness. During his conversation with Peter, Jesus told the parable of the unforgiving servant (Mt 18:23-35). Luke's gospel has a series of five forgiveness parables: the barren fig tree (Lk 13:6-9); the bent-over woman (Lk 13:10-13); the lost sheep (Lk 15:4-7); the lost coin (Lk15:8-10); and the greatest forgiveness parable of all, the prodigal son (Lk 15:11-32).

Jesus was extremely kind and merciful in the way that he forgave those who sinned against others. Jesus told the paralytic, "Child, your sins are forgiven" (Mk 2:5); when a sinful woman bathed Jesus' feet with her tears and wiped them with her hair, Jesus said, "Your sins are forgiven" (Lk 7:48); when a woman caught in adultery was brought before him, he said, "I do not condemn you" (Jn 8:11); and as Jesus hung on the cross he told the repentant criminal, "Today you will be with me in paradise" (Lk 23:43).

5) **Committed**

Jesus had no lack of commitment whatsoever. Wherever He was, or whoever He was with, He was fully in the moment and fully committed to His goals. Despite praying fervently in the garden of Gethsemane to avoid having to bear the cross and all that physical torture, He knew it was the only way to pay for everyone's sins, so He stayed completely committed to His goal. There were certainly many obstacles during His ministry, but He stayed on track and finished strong. How committed are you as a child of God, many will argue that Afterall I am not a church worker, we have a mandate to be fruitful and our fruit must abide, how many souls have you won into the body of Christ since you were saved, some are yet to win a soul, it's not too late fall in line and do the needful and the Lord will open the flood gate of blessings before you. The reward is sure, and you will receive it in Jesus name. John 15:4-6, 'Abide in Me, and I in you. As the branch cannot bear fruit of itself, unless it abides in the vine, neither can you, unless you abide in Me. "I am the vine, you are the branches. He who abides in Me, and I in him, bears much fruit; for without Me you can do nothing. 6 If anyone does not abide in Me, he is cast out as a branch and is withered; and they gather them and throw them into the fire, and they are burned', this scripture is applicable to every believer and once you are committed to bearing fruits for the lord and if such fruits abide, the Lord delivers a blank cheque for you when you fulfil the part of the deal, verse 7 of John 15 says, 'If you abide in Me, and My words abide in you, you[a] will ask what you desire, and it shall be done for you.', can you imagine the blessings that will follow and express answers to prayer.

In John 13:31-38, Jesus gives three distinguishing marks of a committed Christian. Remember, Jesus' earthly ministry was coming to an end. It was the night before His death. And He was spending those last hours with His disciples to prepare them for His leaving. He had just dismissed Judas to leave His presence eternally. With Judas gone, Jesus turned to the eleven remaining disciples and gave them a valedictory address, a farewell speech.

Therefore when [Judas] had gone out, Jesus said, "Now is the Son of Man glorified, and God is glorified in Him; if God is glorified in Him, God will also glorify Him in Himself and will glorify Him immediately. Little children, I am with you a little while longer. You will seek Me; and as I said to the Jews, now I also say to you, 'Where I am going, you cannot come.' A new commandment I give to you, that you love one another, even as I have loved you, that you also love one another. By this, all men will know that you are My disciples if you have a love for one another."

Simon Peter said to Him, "Lord, where are You going?" Jesus answered, "Where I go, you cannot follow Me now; but you shall follow later." Peter said to Him, "Lord, why can I not follow You right now? I will lay down my life for you." Jesus answered, "Will you lay down your life for Me? Truly, truly, I say to you, a rooster will not crow until you deny Me three times."

This passage introduces Jesus' last commission to His disciples before He went to the cross. His farewell message, which continues through John 16, contains every ingredient we need to know about discipleship. In fact, the basics of Paul's teaching about discipleship come right out of this portion of John. Thus these concluding words of our Lord on His last evening with His disciples are strategic to our understanding of what Christ expects of us as believers. Here Jesus gives three distinguishing marks of a committed Christian. These ingredients should be evident in the life of every disciple.

6) **Prayerful**

No matter how busy His ministry got, He found time to be alone and pray. Whether it is in the garden of Gethsemane, across a river, or on a mountaintop, Jesus disappeared for a while in order to pray to the Lord. People always tried to find Him, and He never turned them away, but He also made sure to make time spent with His heavenly Father a priority. In Christendom today we are very lazy when it comes to prayer, most of us only pray when we are in crises, the bible says in 1 Thessalonian 5:17, 'Pray without ceasing.' No matter what the situation is, good or bad ensure you pray and could mean the following:

a) Spirit of Dependence

First, it means that there is a spirit of dependence that should permeate all we do. This is the very spirit and essence of prayer: dependence. So, even when we are not speaking consciously to God, there is a deep, abiding dependence on him that is woven into the very essence of our faith.

In that sense, we are praying. We are experiencing a spirit of dependence continuously, and that kind of disposition is, I think, right at the heart of what God creates when he creates a Christian.

b) Repeated and Frequent

The second meaning that it has (and I think this is probably the one that is foremost in Paul's conscious intention here) is that praying without ceasing means praying repeatedly and often. I base that on the way he used the word unceasing (Greek adialeiptōs) in Romans 1:9. Listen to how he uses the same word for without ceasing. He says, "For God is my witness, whom I serve with my spirit in the gospel of his Son, that without ceasing [adialeiptōs] I mention you."

Now, we can be sure that Paul did not make mention of the Romans in every minute or second of his prayers or his days or his preaching. He prayed and he spoke about lots of other things besides the Romans. But he mentioned them over and over. He mentioned them often. He mentioned them regularly. So he says, "I mentioned you without ceasing."

It doesn't mean that he was verbally and mentally always, every second, mentioning them. It means that over and over, always, repeatedly, without fail, when I get on my knees, you are in my prayer. That is basically what I think he means by "pray without ceasing" — repeatedly and often.

c) Staying Steadfast

The third thing I think he means is this: not giving up on prayer. "Without ceasing" means you should never come to a point in your life when you say, "Prayer doesn't work. I am done. I am giving up on prayer." That would be the very opposite of "without ceasing." It means, "Don't ever do that. Don't ever get to that point." So, the key to rejoicing always is to pray continually — that is, to lean on God all the time and to call him repeatedly and often. Never give up looking to him for help. Come to him repeatedly during the day, and come often. Make the default state of your mind a Godward longing and a Godward thankfulness. We must ensure that our prayer life is improved. This is the only way we can communicate with God.

7) **Gentleness**

There were certainly times where Jesus used stern words, but He knew when gentleness was appropriate. Children seemed to love coming to him, and He made sure the disciples knew not to hinder them when they did so. When speaking with His disciples, mother, or other ladies, He could be very kind-hearted and gentle. But, when He was giving someone a rebuke or making a point in an argument, He knew when turning up the heat as necessary and only did so strategically.

Most of the world's literature and entertainment has exalted the conquering hero who refuses to submit, and who exerts his or her interests against anyone who might challenge those interests. Most of the world's cultures have reserved their rewards for people who compete successfully through the strength of will and superior power. In contrast, the meek and gentle person is ridiculed for being weak and soft, and of no real value in society.

Often, the most rewarded salespeople are those with the most aggressive methods. The politicians most often voted into office are usually the biggest liars and the most ruthless of men and women. Today, frequently, the heads of large corporations are those who have robbed others blind, stolen secrets, and cheated people of their retirement funds. In such a context, Jesus portrays the ideal disciple as someone who is meek and gentle. The promised reward that such a person will inherit the earth is a bold contradiction of worldly wisdom.

There is a clear distinction between existence in the world, and worldly conduct and methods. There is no denying that all Christians have human weaknesses, but we know that spiritual warfare demands spiritual weapons. We can wage a successful campaign in the spiritual realm only as worldly weapons are abandoned. Total reliance must be placed on the spiritual weaponry, which is divinely effective for demolishing seemingly impregnable evil strongholds and defending the ongoing attacks.

In this society today, as in the society of the first century, these evil strongholds that crumble before the weapons of the spirit are such things as intellectualism and traditions of men. Paul calls these "the wisdom of this world." Around 55-56 AD, Paul had been accused of being forceful and bold shooting his printed arrows at a distance, but subservient and weak-kneed when personally present, weakly voicing his demands. To this accusation he replied:

2 Corinthians 10:8-10, For even if I should boast somewhat more about our authority, which the Lord gave us for edification and not for your destruction, I shall not be ashamed—lest I seem to terrify you by letters. "For his letters," they say, "are weighty and powerful, but his bodily presence is weak, and his speech contemptible." This charge is a repeat of what Paul used as his prelude to chapter 10, "I, Paul, myself am pleading with you." He took that gentle approach. He was stating this regarding a vocal minority who persisted in thinking that worldly standards and motives

governed all his conduct and that he relied on human powers and methods in his ministry. They basically placed him on a physical level using physical tactics.

Paul wanted to avoid a display of boldness on his upcoming visit. Yet, he indicates his total readiness to exercise his authority if they would not refuse to listen to his slanderers and change their own attitudes toward God's minister. Paul preferred to come to Corinth "with love, in a spirit of gentleness" but, if necessary, he was ready to come, rod in hand. So, it was left up to the congregation, in one sense, how he would approach them, whether it would be gentle or stern. Paul addresses the whole church on this issue. He explains that his war, and theirs, is a spiritual war. Right at the beginning of this passage, Paul uses two words that set the whole tone of his purpose in writing this chapter. He writes of "the meekness and gentleness of Christ."

2 Corinthians 10:1 Now I, Paul, myself am pleading with you by the meekness and gentleness of Christ—who in presence am lowly among you, but being absent am bold toward you. So, Paul's meekness and gentleness as a servant of Christ should not be confused with timidity. He was not a timid person. He had quite a bit of authority and forcefulness in his mannerism, but he also had that side of gentleness that he needed in instructing members of the church.

2 Corinthians 10:2-5 But I beg you that when I am present I may not be bold with that confidence by which I intend to be bold against some, who think of us as if we walked according to the flesh. For though we walk in the flesh, we do not war according to the flesh. For the weapons of our warfare are not carnal but mighty in God for pulling down strongholds, casting down arguments and every high thing that exalts itself against the knowledge of God, bringing every thought into captivity to the obedience of Christ.

Paul uses the phrase "every high thing" here in verse 5. In some translations, it is translated "every pretension," referring to any human act or attitude that forms an obstacle to the liberating knowledge of God contained in His inspired written Word. In this, Paul is referring to every arrogant plot or presumptuous design that temporarily frustrates God's divine plan. We know nothing frustrates God Himself as He carries out His plan of salvation for humanity. The frustration is on the part of human beings who allow themselves to be deceived, or influenced, by human reasoning and Satan's wiles.

Paul, who was formerly a zealous persecutor of the church, recognizes that gentleness does not come naturally for many. He explicitly lists gentleness, or meekness, as a fruit of the Spirit, a virtue that is planted and flourishes where God dwells by His Spirit. Meekness is listed in Galatians 5:23 as the eighth fruit of the Spirit in the King James Version. But, it is translated gentleness in most modern English translations. This is not a matter of any difference in the ancient Greek manuscripts of the New Testament. The Greek word practise is found in all the translations. The problem here is that the English language has changed since the days of King James and Shakespeare. The common dictionary definition of meekness as it is used today is deficient in spirit and courage. Over time, this etymology has moved away from the original Greek meaning.

Meekness is an elusive virtue, in that few people know how to define it. Most definitions are vague on its meaning and many people incorrectly equate it to weakness. Meekness is inclusive of such virtues as humble, mild, gentle, modest, unassuming, unpretentious, tolerant, tender-hearted. We get a feel of its general meaning. In English, "meek" comes from the Old Norse word mjuker, meaning soft. You see there where the English of meekness has come to mean soft or weak.

In modern English, the terms meekness and mildness, which are commonly used for this Greek word, suggest weakness and cowardliness to a greater or lesser extent. But, the Greek word prautes does not express this. The meekness manifested by God and given to the saints is the fruit of power. It is an enduring injury with patience and without resentment. Resentment is a feeling of indignant displeasure or persistent ill will at something regarded as a wrong, an insult, or an injury. The spirit of God cannot dwell in the heart of someone who is harsh or resentful. Meekness and gentleness are to be "put on" with other Christian virtues such as compassion, lowliness, and patience as Paul taught the saints and faithful brethren of the church in Colossae.

Even though there were arrogant people in the church at Corinth, gentleness was Paul's preferred means of dealing with them. I Corinthians 4:21 What do you want? Shall I come to you with a rod, or in love and a spirit of gentleness? Paul had a tremendous love for the faithful in all the congregations of God, but his love was not mere blind sentimentality. He knew they sometimes needed discipline, and he was prepared to use it. But, he wanted to see them respond in repentance so he could show them the meekness and gentleness of Christ in his approach. That was always his preferred approach.

In speaking of his ministry among the Thessalonians, Paul's gentleness takes on a maternal image. I Thessalonians 2:7 But we were gentle among you, just as a nursing mother cherishes her own children. You see there an indication of how the ministry should deal with the members of the church. Just as a mother who cherishes her own children does. Remember where Paul's, and our, meekness and gentleness originated. We already read the answer in II Corinthians. 2 Corinthians 10:1 "Now I, Paul, myself am pleading with you by the meekness [Greek prauteetos] and gentleness [Greek epieikeias] of Christ."

Then he goes on to talk about the weapons of the world. On the contrary, we have divine power to tear down evil strongholds. We are not carried away by rage, personal vindictiveness, greed, or pride. But, with the gentleness of Christ, we can triumph powerfully. Gentleness is one of the spiritual weapons that we use against those sins of the world that are so harsh.

Remain on Track

Meekness and gentleness appear in the Bible among lists of virtues, and two corresponding themes are associated with them. God commands us to behave that way and rewards are promised to people who display these virtues of meekness and gentleness. How do meekness and gentleness relate to one another? Meekness is both internal and external in its execution in one's life. Gentleness is one of the best English words to express the outward operation of meekness. 2 Corinthians 10:1 refers to Christ's meekness (prauteetos) and gentleness (epieikeia). They are indicated as separate virtues that Christ has and that we should desire. Meekness describes a condition of the mind and heart—an internal attitude—whereas gentleness describes mildness combined with tenderness. It refers to actions, that is, external behaviour. They go hand in hand, they work together. Described negatively, meekness is the opposite of self-assertiveness and self-interest; it is evenness of mind that is neither elated nor cast down, simply because it is not occupied with self at all.

Gentleness is never a false modesty, a self-depreciation, or a spineless refusal to stand for anything. It is never a cowardly retreat from reality that substitutes passive selfishness for true gentleness and avoids trouble in ways that allow even greater trouble to develop. Neither is it a false humility that refuses to recognize that God has given us talents and abilities, or that refuses to use them for His glory. Meekness is a virtue that Christians are commanded to put on and aim for, and we are repeatedly exhorted to be meek and gentle.

Meekness and gentleness are commanded as the spirit in which we are called to perform certain duties as Christians. The list of such duties includes restoring badly behaving Christians, correcting opponents of the truth, receiving the implanted word, and making a defence of the gospel. These are all ways that gentleness or meekness are used. Let me pose a rhetorical question. Do you know someone with a fault? That is an easy question to answer as we can all think of people with faults.

Should we condemn and judge, or recall the mercy God the Father and Jesus Christ have had on us? Let us briefly look at four passages that answer these questions. These are self-explanatory and will give you a good overall answer to this. Galatians 6:1 Brethren, if a man is overtaken in any trespass, you who are spiritual restore such a one in a spirit of gentleness, considering yourself lest you also be tempted. 2 Timothy 2:23-26 But avoid foolish and ignorant disputes, knowing that they generate strife. And a servant of the Lord must not quarrel but be gentle to all, able to teach, patient, in humility correcting those who are in opposition, if God perhaps will grant them repentance, so that they may know the truth, and that they may come to their senses and escape the snare of the devil, having been taken captive by him to do his will.

These are all verses that tell us how we should deal with others having to do with such things as restoring a badly behaving Christian, correcting opponents of the truth, and receiving the implanted word. James 1:19-21 So then, my beloved brethren, let every man be swift to hear, slow to speak, slow to wrath; for the wrath of man does not produce the righteousness of God. Therefore lay aside all filthiness and overflow of wickedness, and receive with meekness the implanted word, which is able to save your souls.

In this next scripture, we will see making a defence for the gospel is another reason or time when we use meekness or gentleness. I Peter 3:15-16 But sanctify the Lord God in your hearts, and always be ready to give a defence to everyone who asks you a reason for the hope that is in you, with meekness and fear; having a good conscience, that when they defame you as evildoers, those who revile your good conduct in Christ may be ashamed. So we see nature or the attitude which we take such accusations and defaming.

Gentleness is the spirit in which to learn and in which discipline must be applied and faults corrected. It is also the virtue for meeting opposition to the truth and giving a proper Christian witness. I do not know how many times during the last forty years or so that I have come across men who decided that they were going to ram the truth down someone's throat rather than giving it to them in a meek and gentle way. Right off the bat, they have alienated the person to listening to anything further. I think that is a very common mistake that zealots, so to speak, make.

We should not try to cram God's truth down the throats of people in the world. The best way for us to witness Christ and to glorify God is to live God's way of life, providing a good example to others. Biblically, the focus of true meekness and gentleness is not only in our outward behaviour, nor in our relationships to other human beings, neither is it the focus of our natural personality. Rather it is an inwardly developed tenderheartedness, and the performing of it is first and primarily towards God. It is the attitude in which we accept God's will toward us as good, and therefore without disputing or resisting. That is the true focus of meekness and gentleness.

Since true meekness is meekness before God, the insults and injuries that may be inflicted on us by the world, or others within the church, are permitted and used by God for our chastening and purifying. It is impossible to have true unity without meekness and gentleness. Remember, meekness is an enduring injury with patience and without resentment. Gentleness is a softness of manner and disposition. There is an absence of harshness, fierceness, or violence in it.

We cannot be unified unless we come to the point, on an individual basis, where we are no longer bothered by the intentional or unintentional offences from others—especially our spiritual brothers and sisters. We see an indication of how important meekness is for our future in Matthew 5:5 where Jesus Christ says: "Blessed are the meek, for they shall inherit the earth." The two biblical characters, with whom we most readily associate meekness, are Moses and Jesus.

We read in Numbers 12:3 regarding Moses that he "was very humble, [meek] more than all men that were on the face of the earth." If we examine the life of Moses, we find good evidence that meekness is not weakness, but strength under control. There is no more heroic and forceful character in the Old Testament than Moses. He is fearless in exercising leadership against unbearable intransigence among his followers. He stands up to Pharaoh. He defends his right to lead when his authority is challenged. He is the most visible and powerful figure in the travelling nation of Israel.

Yet, he does all this in the strength of God, and he himself makes no presumption to be self-reliant, nor does he use his position as leader for self-aggrandizement. The major exception is when he strikes the rock instead of obeying God's command to speak to it, accompanied by self-importance about being the one to bring forth the water. He said, "Hear now, you rebels! Must we bring water for you out of this rock?" Where was his credit to God? So, even Moses made mistakes. The inappropriateness of Moses' behaviour on this occasion, compared with the general tone of his whole life, works to emphasize the great effort it takes to produce the quality of meekness and gentleness even in a person with God's Holy Spirit.

"Gentleness" describes the person who is so much in control of himself that he is always angry at the right time and never angry at the wrong time, just like Moses, who God praised for being the meekest among his contemporaries. Though one of the greatest leaders in human history, he thought of himself as a servant in relation to God, so he quietly submitted to God's will. He refused to elevate his own importance over that of God, using his authority in humility. In doing that, having a humble attitude, he was able to have a gentle approach.

Protestants teach their children a prayer, "Gentle Jesus, meek and mild." But, in the New Testament, Jesus is never described as weak, or mild, as the prayer indicates. That word meek, that they use in that prayer, really in their minds means weak. Jesus was sometimes quite the opposite, both forceful and authoritative. While discerning the Pharisees' harsh, hypocritical intentions Jesus called them "brood of vipers." He also overturned the tables of the money changers at the synagogue. Matthew 21:12-14 Then Jesus went into the temple of God and drove out all those who bought and sold in the temple and overturned the tables of the money-changers and the seats of those who sold doves. And He said to them, "It is written, 'My house shall be called a house of prayer,' but you have made it a 'den of thieves.' Then the blind and the lame came to Him in the temple, and He healed them.

So, between verse 13 and verse 14 we see the two strong sides of Jesus' personality and character. On the one side, He was very forceful, steadfast, and authoritative. But then right away, He becomes gentle. Matthew 21:15-17 But when the chief priests and scribes saw the wonderful things that He did, and the children crying out in the temple and saying, "Hosanna to the Son of David!" they were indignant and said to Him, "Do You hear what these are saying?" And Jesus said to them, "Yes. Have you never read, 'Out of the mouth of babes and nursing infants You have perfected praise'?" Then He left them and went out of the city to Bethany, and He lodged there. So, we see there a contrast between Christ's gentle approach, but with authority, and the Pharisees' harsh, condemning approach. A weak and mild Jesus is not biblical. But gentle Jesus is! Jesus Himself says so. In Jesus' many statements about Himself, one of the most memorable is found in Matthew 11:28-30 Come to Me, all you who labour and are heavy laden, and I will give you rest. "Take My yoke upon you and learn from Me, for I am gentle and lowly in heart, and you will find rest for your souls. "For My yoke is easy and My burden is light."

Gentleness is a God-like quality and was strongly evident in the life of Jesus Christ. He gathered children about Him—they sat on His knee and He took time to converse with them. When the disciples sought to dismiss them as a nuisance, Jesus rebuked them. Matthew 19:13-14 Then little children were brought to Him that He might put His hands on them and pray, but the disciples rebuked them. But Jesus said, "Let the little children come to Me, and do not forbid them; for of such is the kingdom of heaven."

Jesus often demonstrated the character traits of meekness and gentleness. Here are another five brief examples: It is seen in his treatment of the woman caught in adultery that the Pharisees wanted to stone.

The way he treated Thomas, who refused to believe that Jesus had risen from the dead until he saw Jesus with his own eyes. The way in which he associated with the outcasts of society, the sinners, the prostitutes, and the tax collectors.

The way in which he healed people who were suffering. His conversation with the woman at the well in Samaria. Jesus engaged her in conversation that drew her in rather than alienating her. He allowed her to admit her sin rather than condemning her from the start. The conversation was a gentle conversation that went very well. No doubt that lady remembered that, and who knows, maybe she was converted.

We can learn from all of these examples how to properly communicate with others of varying backgrounds. Although Jesus is the truly powerful one, and the truly righteous one, He was gentle for the benefit of the weak and the blind sinners. A memorable example of Jesus' show of meekness and gentleness was during his arrest. When he was being arrested in the Garden of Gethsemane, one of his disciples, Peter, pulled out a sword and struck Malchus, the servant of the high priest, cutting off his ear. Matthew 26:52-53 But Jesus said to him, "Put your sword in its place, for all who take the sword will perish by the sword. "Or do you think that I cannot now pray to My Father, and He will provide Me with more than twelve legions of angels?

You can hear his firmness, but that gentleness in what He told Peter. Jesus had massive strength at His disposal, but He restrained His use of power because He knew that He must die to bring salvation to the weak. He put aside the strength and power of a king and in meekness, not weakness, for the benefit of the weak demonstrates the kind of King He is—not a domineering tyrant, but a meek and gentle King, although supremely powerful.

He is the King of kings who entered Jerusalem, riding on a donkey. Matthew 21:1-11 Now when they drew near Jerusalem, and came to Bethphage, at the Mount of Olives, then Jesus sent two disciples, saying to them, "Go into the village opposite you, and immediately you will find a donkey tied and a colt with her. Lose them and bring them to Me. "And if anyone says anything to you, you shall say, 'The Lord has need of them,' and immediately he will send them." All this was done that it might be fulfilled which was spoken by the prophet, saying: "Tell the daughter of Zion, 'Behold, your King is coming to you, Lowly, and sitting on a donkey, A colt, the foal of a donkey.'" So the disciples went and did as Jesus commanded them. They brought the donkey and the colt, laid their clothes on them, and set Him on them. And a very great multitude spread their clothes on the road; others cut down branches from the trees and spread them on the road. Then the multitudes who went before and those who followed cried out, saying: "Hosanna to the Son of David! 'Blessed is He who comes in the name of the Lord!' Hosanna in the highest!" And when He had come into Jerusalem, all the city was moved, saying, "Who is this?" So the multitudes said, "This is Jesus, the prophet from Nazareth of Galilee."

Here, we see the image of the truly meek and gentle leader, teacher, and King. It is interesting because, early on, the disciples thought that He was going to come into Jerusalem with a rod of iron and conquer the city and take over the area so that He could set up His kingship. Later, when Jesus knew, in advance, that Peter would deny Him and Judas would betray Him, He did not rise in angry protest. His gentle nature restrained Him. He commanded that we love our enemies, do good to those who hate us, and subdue our harsh nature with gentleness. Peter himself was inspired to write about how Jesus is the supreme example of meekness and gentleness.

I Peter 2:21-24 For to this you were called, because Christ also suffered for us, leaving us an example, that you should follow His steps: "Who committed no sin, nor was deceit found in His mouth;" who, when He was reviled, did not revile in return; when He suffered, He did not threaten, but committed Himself to Him who judges righteously; who Himself bore our sins in His own body on the tree, that we, having died to sins, might live for righteousness—by whose stripes you were healed.

Defiant toward the religious establishment in defending the helpless and diseased, as well as opposing evil, Jesus is self-effacing in regard to His own interests. From the cross, He prays that His heavenly Father would forgive those who crucify Him. No wonder He characterizes Himself as being "gentle and lowly in heart."

With all this gentleness, He was masculine and firm. When confronted by those seeking to entrap or destroy Him, He stood fearless and His gentle nature was temporarily masked as He demonstrated a strength that struck fear into the hearts of those who heard Him. It is not a mere contemplative virtue; it is maintaining peace and patience during pelting provocations. Isaiah's prophecy summarizes Jesus' example well. Isaiah 53:4 Surely, He has born our griefs and carried our sorrows;

Isaiah 53:7 He was oppressed, and He was afflicted, yet He opened not His mouth; He was led as a lamb to the slaughter, and as a sheep before its shearers is silent, so He opened not His mouth. Isaiah 53:9 And they made His grave with the wicked—because He had done no violence, nor was any deceit in His mouth."

Jesus Christ, gentle and lowly of heart! It is interesting how often the mouth is mentioned there and how He had control of his tongue. Without control of our tongue, we cannot have gentleness. In stark contrast, the disciples of Jesus Christ wanted to burn sinners. They mistakenly thought ferocity was the ideal behaviour for a servant of God. Then God intervened, through Jesus, to show them that they were wrong. In Mark 3, James and John were called the "the Sons of Thunder," a name was given to them by Christ. The Gospel of Luke shows this was an appropriate nickname for the two of them. Jesus and His disciples were travelling to Jerusalem, and on the way, they sought lodging in a Samaritan city. Historians tell us of the long-standing enmity between the Samaritans and the Jews. Samaritans refused to allow Jews to enter their city.

Luke 9 records that because they feel snubbed, James and John say they would like to duplicate Elijah's miracle of 'bringing fire down from heaven' to destroy the Samaritan village. Jesus is obviously repulsed by their attitudes. Luke 9:55-56 But He turned and rebuked them, and said, "You do not know what manner of spirit you are of. "For the Son of Man did not come to destroy men's lives but to save them." And they went to another village.

Jesus sets James and John straight in their attitudes, and His unequivocal response comes through in His statement that "He turned and rebuked them." Jesus lets James and John know that their attitude should be one of meekness and gentleness. He reminds them of His reason for coming: "the Son of Man did not come to destroy men's lives, but to save them." Here, we see the main reason for "gentleness" in dealing with people—not to destroy people's lives or humiliate them.

This biblical account of the "Sons of Thunder" emphasizes that we are to be predominately gentle Christians, just as our Saviour, Jesus Christ, was gentle. But, with the right balance of that firmness and that steadfastness in the truth. As human beings, it is so hard for us to get the right balance. James eventually came to understand what Jesus meant by His statement, "I am gentle and lowly in heart." When James speaks of the wisdom "from above" he refers to it as "meek" or "gentle."

James 3:13 Who is wise and understanding among you? Let him show by good conduct that his works are done in the meekness of wisdom. Regarding the phrase "meekness of wisdom" in verse 13, Barnes' Notes has this comment: A wise and prudent gentleness of life; not in a noisy, arrogant, and boastful manner. True wisdom is always meek, mild, gentle; and that is the wisdom which is needful if men would become public teachers. It is remarkable that the truly wise man is always characterized by a calm spirit, a mild and placid demeanour, and by a gentle, though firm, enunciation of his sentiments. A noisy, boisterous, and stormy declaimer we never select as a safe counsellor. He may accomplish much in his way by his bold eloquence of manner, but we do not put him in places where we need far-reaching thought, or where we expect the exercise of profound philosophical views. In an eminent degree, the ministry of the gospel should be characterized by a calm, gentle, and thoughtful wisdom —a wisdom which shines in all the actions of the life.

James contrasts this meek and gentle "wisdom from above" with envious and self-seeking "worldly wisdom." James 3:14-17 But if you have bitter envy and self-seeking in your hearts, do not boast and lie against the truth. This wisdom does not descend from above but is earthly, sensual, and demonic. For where envy and self-seeking exist, confusion and every evil thing are there. But the wisdom that is from above is first pure, then peaceable, gentle, willing to yield, full of mercy and good fruits, without partiality and without hypocrisy.

Gentleness should be an ever-present restraint in all our thoughts and actions. It comes to some men seemingly by inheritance. To most, however, it must be developed, since it is generally lacking. Our firm, masculine nature does not encourage these gentle qualities. This society has been negligent in portraying proper gentle behaviour in men, except as it is portrayed as a quality in homosexually perverted men. And, of course, we realize that Satan perverts everything, especially godly character qualities.

Satan has perverted gentleness in men by convincing some men that an outward softness with an effeminate slant is an admirable quality.

But, the heart of the homosexual is bent on self-destruction resulting from his lifestyle. Statistics show that homosexual men have a very short life span compared with, in the modern vernacular, "straight men."

The mind of the homosexual is twisted with lusts for power and control over others, paedophilia, and disloyalty. The promotion of perverted "Man-Boy Love" associations and websites shows the aggressiveness and militancy of this twisted movement. Crime, child abuse, and multiple sex partners are strikingly high among this group. The homosexual's lifestyle is one of self-gratification and there is nothing gentle about it. Among the rest of society, because gentleness is strong in the feminine nature, many men avoid being gentle, thinking it a mark of femininity and softness. Men who lack such qualities as strength, endurance, confidence, decisiveness, assertiveness, and self-control tend to swallow the macho, out-of-control image promoted by the media. The fashion their lives to be like that and they imitate their heroes of the big screen.

In the Christian man, God carefully blends gentleness with firm masculinity to produce an attractive combination in a man that is striking and admirable. His gentleness must be acquired by subduing his masculine human nature as one would tame a wild colt. Our passionate feelings must be controlled, and our harsh temperament restrained. So, we get back to it being a matter of self-control.

Aubrey Andelin, in his book Man of Steel and Velvet, illustrates gentleness this way:

Gentleness is to the steel qualities what mercy is to justice. When justice is meted out alone, it is cold, undeviating, and unsympathetic. Although justice is in reality given for the benefit of the individual, without mercy it appears intent on the suffering or even the destruction of the person. As mercy softens justice, gentleness softens the steel in man. I thought he put that very well.

Women especially need the combination of the gentleness of velvet and the firmness of steel. Children also require gentleness constantly. A gentle voice, kindly manner, and soft expression build good relationships with children, along with firmness in upholding righteous standards. All gentleness will make nothing but an extortionist because your child will exhort what he wants out of you, and out of society later.

Many men lack this gentleness of spirit, much to the pain of their families. Sometimes, we fathers expect more righteousness in our children than we do of ourselves. They do not have God's Holy Spirit—as we do—helping us to produce spiritual fruit such as gentleness. We want our children to avoid the mistakes that we made, but sometimes we expect more perfection from them than they can produce. We end up frustrated, and they end up discouraged. The gentleman passes by dissatisfaction in his children and sees their progress, rather than their failures. A positive gentle approach in raising our children becomes an encouraging and enjoyable bonding, between father and child, and mother and child.

Nevertheless, occasional "anger-less" corporal punishment is necessary according to the biblical instruction for serious infractions. The wisest man who ever lived was inspired to record this divine instruction in Proverbs 22:15: "Foolishness is bound up in the heart of a child, but the rod of correction will drive it far from him." That is scriptural, and anyone who disagrees with what God has inspired there can take it up with God. But, remember there must be that gentle side in carrying out correction. Combine this with the gentle approach in childrearing and the result is that a child's spirit is guided, rather than broken.

Godly love requires a gentle nature, so we cannot hope to teach it to our children unless we demonstrate it ourselves. They will not listen to our instruction if we fail to win their hearts with a gentle disposition. Yes, we can demand their obedience and we should. But our firmness must be controlled with gentleness.

In many of the passages that enjoin meekness or gentleness as a virtue, it is easy to get the impression that this virtue is displayed especially in speech, a principle made explicitly in Proverbs 15:4 that "a wholesome [or as the ESV says, gentle] tongue is a tree of life." Marriage problems often start with harsh words. Sometimes harsh words show up very early in the marriage. Paul gives us advice on the character of the new man that can greatly improve our relationships with not only our spouses but with all personal relationships.

Colossians 3:12-13 Therefore, as the elect of God, holy and beloved, put on tender mercies, kindness, humility, meekness, longsuffering;

bearing with one another, and forgiving one another, if anyone has a complaint against another; even as Christ forgave you, so you also must do. It has been said, that the meek are those who give soft answers to tough questions.

In Proverbs 15, we find two striking images of gentleness that show its disarming power. Proverbs 15:1 "A soft [gentle] answer turns away wrath, but a harsh word stirs up anger." If we are prone to pronounce threats we miss the point of our calling. Humiliating, harsh comments do not reflect the values of the Bible. As the prophet Isaiah wrote:

Isaiah 50:4 "The Lord God has given Me the tongue of the learned, that I should know how to speak a word in season to him who is weary. He awakens Me morning by morning, He awakens My ear to hear as the learned.

This scripture is a prophecy of Jesus Christ, our example. The book of Isaiah shows us that Jesus Christ will deal with us with the utmost tenderness and gentleness. Isaiah 40:11 He will feed His flock like a shepherd; He will gather the lambs with His arm, and carry them in His bosom, and gently lead those who are with young.

Gentleness is the spirit of humility and does not consider itself too good, or too exalted, for humble tasks. Meekness is recognizing our smallness before Almighty God. With this attitude, we will esteem our spouses better than ourselves. What is your attitude toward your wife or husband? Do you feel better than her or him? Even more telling, what do your actions show? An attitude of pride and superiority must be changed if a marriage is to thrive. Marriages sometimes survive under these conditions. They would not thrive, that is improving and get better as the years go by.

A husband must allow the Spirit of God to lead him to place his wife above himself. She is not inferior to him. God created both man and woman in His image. When God created life upon the earth, He made human beings the pinnacle of the physical creation, fashioned in His own image. This is sometimes included in the marriage ceremony. He gave men and women a spirit, and creative minds with the ability to make choices, to develop plans, and to build their lives upon them.

Men and women were created with the marvellous potential of eternal life in the family of God. And as a loving Father, God gave us the institution of marriage and the blessing of the family that we might learn to love one another as He loves us, and thus be created in His character image. After He had created the first man from the dust of the ground, the Lord God said, "It is not good that man should be alone; I will make him a helper comparable to him." (Genesis 2:18)

The woman was made equal to the man in spiritual potential, the perfect complement to her husband. To emphasize His purpose to Adam and Eve, the Creator did not make the woman directly from the dust, but from the very flesh and bone of the man. When the woman was presented to him, Adam said, "This is now bone of my bones and flesh of my flesh." So, how do we treat our own bones and flesh? Do we treat it harshly? Well, some do, those who smoke and take drugs. But, the right way to treat our own bodies is with gentleness and we certainly should treat our spouses with gentleness.

In I Peter 3:7, Peter wrote that husbands should give honour to his wife, as to the weaker vessel. Peter used the word "honour." This word gives positive direction to the whole verse. Peter speaks of a structurally weaker vessel that has esteem and value. A wife could be compared to a delicate yet beautiful piece of crystal. We put the fine crystal in a showcase. We give it an honour. Structurally, a husband could be compared to a strong vessel—maybe something like stainless steel. Just as crystal, it will not rust or corrode. If husbands and wives esteem each other better than themselves, they would automatically treat each other gently and with more respect. Feelings and actions of inferiority and superiority would not exist in that type of marriage. Gentleness requires the existence of love.

In Ephesians 4, Paul urges us to live a life worthy of the calling we have received, he calls on us to be completely humble and gentle. Ephesians 4:2 "With all lowliness and gentleness, with longsuffering, bearing with one another in love." We are to be free from self-exaltation and fully submitted to the will of God both in our relationship with Him and in our relationship with our spouse. The apostle Peter was inspired to write that "a quiet and gentle spirit" among wives is "in God's sight—very precious."

I Peter 3:3-4 Do not let your adornment be merely outward adorning of arranging the hair, of wearing gold, or of putting on fine apparel; rather let it be the hidden person of the heart, with the incorruptible ornament of a gentle and quiet spirit, which is very precious in the sight of God. I Peter 3:7-8 Likewise you husbands, dwell with them with understanding, giving honour to the wife, as to the weaker vessel, and as being heirs together of the grace of life, that your prayers may not be hindered. Finally, all of you be of one mind, having compassion for one another; love as brothers, be tender-hearted, be courteous.

These are all elements of meekness and gentleness. They are strongly positive virtues, and not a display of passive timidity. We can understand them more clearly if we list the behaviours they are not. "Meekness and gentleness" are the opposite of harshness, vengefulness, self-aggrandizement, and lack of self-control. The key to understanding these virtues is that they are not qualities of weakness, but rather of strength. They are not cowardice, timidity, or a lack of confidence. Meekness and gentleness imply self-control; therefore, they require strength under control. The qualities of meekness and gentleness stand in the Bible as the proper temperament for a servant of God.

King David was an impressive example of strength and gentleness. As a young shepherd boy, he slew both a lion and a bear. With only a sling and a pebble from a brook, he killed the feared Goliath. He led armies and governed a kingdom. And yet he had a gentle nature. He loved music and wrote poetry. He spoke of fruit in its season, of mouths of babes and nursing infants, of roses and lambs, of green pastures and still waters. David was a man after God's own heart. He was steadfast and gentle, but he had to develop his gentleness over time because he was a very war-like man throughout much of his life.

What can we do to subdue a harsh nature and develop gentleness? Aubrey Andelin, in his book Man of Steel and Velvet, suggests three things. I thought this was very good advice:

We must work to have restraint and self-control. We must bring our actions and emotions under control. We should bridle our tongues as one would bridle a horse and lead it where it should go. We have to train our feelings to react righteously and restrain and subdue any harshness in our temperaments.

We must work to develop a gentle character. Our harsh conduct can be brought under control by restraint, but we will never be gentle in nature until there is a change that takes place within our character—until we have a gentle character that automatically prompts us to deal kindly with people. Gentleness comes as we grow spiritually. As we develop love and forgiveness and learn to concentrate on people's virtues rather than their faults, we develop gentleness. We must develop humility. The key to humility is in learning to see our own mistakes and weakness. When this occurs, we soften our attitude toward the errors of others. For example, we may become irritated if a child breaks a lamp or spills paint on the floor. This can cause a harsh attitude to well up towards the child. But, when we consider that we make mistakes probably more serious, despite the fact that we are adults with years of experience, we are humbled and it becomes easier to face the mistakes that others make with a gentle attitude.

In Jesus' message to His disciples in Matthew 5, commonly called the Sermon on the Mount, Jesus honours meek and gentle people: "Blessed are the poor in spirit," "Blessed are the meek," "Blessed are the merciful," "Blessed are the pure in heart," "Blessed are the peacemakers." All of those have elements of gentleness in them. A gentle and quiet spirit is very precious in the sight of God.

8) **Patience**

Throughout the gospels, Jesus clearly gets portrayed as a very patient man. After all, He was surrounded by disciples who constantly doubted him, Pharisees and Sadducees who continually attacked Him, and large crowds who wouldn't leave Him alone. Despite all of that, He kept His composure and responded appropriately to every individual.

"BUT the Lord direct your hearts into the Love of God and into the Patience of Christ" (2 Thess. 3:5). With these words, Paul exhorted the Thessalonian believers. They had many trials and difficulties. They suffered persecutions and were troubled. False alarms had affected their patience of hope in the Lord Jesus Christ. The inspired exhortation puts before their hearts the Patience of Christ. Comfort and joy, encouragement and peace, would surely come to their hearts and strengthen them if they remembered and entered the Patience of Christ.

And who can describe or speak fully and worthily of the Patience of our blessed Lord! It includes so much. His moral Glory and Divine perfections are concealed and revealed in this Word. The word patience has a wide meaning. It means more than we generally express by it. Submission, endurance in meekness, waiting in faith, quietness, contentment, composure, forbearance, suffering in calmness, calmness in suffering; all and more is contained in the one word, Patience. And such patience in all its fullness and perfection the Son of God exhibited in His earthly life. Whenever we look in the Gospels, we behold this calm, quiet, restful patience. His whole life here on earth is but a continued record of patience. In patience, His childhood was spent, and when in His twelfth year the Glory of His Deity flashed forth we read "He went down with them, and came to Nazareth, and was subject unto them." In patience, He whose mighty power had called the universe in existence, toiled on, content in Nazareth, submissive to the Father, till after many years the day would come, when the work

He had come to do should be begun and finished. To describe that Patience during His public ministry from Nazareth, where He had been brought up, to Golgotha, would necessitate scrutiny of every step of the way, every act and every utterance which came from His holy lips. What discoveries of His Grace and moral Glory we make, if under the guidance of His Spirit we meditate on His life here below. Humility and submission under God, patient waiting on Him, the utter absence of all haste, perfect calmness of soul and every other characteristic of perfect patience, we can trace constantly in that wonderful life. What patience is revealed in the forty days in the wilderness, when He hungered and was with the wild beasts (Mark i:13). When Satan tempted Him and asked for stones to be made bread, He exhibited still His patience. In His service, that marvellous service rendered by the perfect servant, no ambitiousness or ostentatiousness can ever be discovered. He pleased not Himself but Him who sent Him. He was constantly going about doing the Father's will. His kindness and love were rewarded by rejection and insults, yet no complaint or murmur ever came from His lips. He was always trusting in God, perfectly calm, perfectly satisfied.

And how His patience shines out in dealing with men. What patience He had with His disciples and how He bore with them in love. They were slow learners. What patience and tenderness in his conversation with her, whom He had sought, the woman at Samaria's well. And greatest above all His patience in suffering. He endured the cross. When He was reviled, He reviled not again; when He suffered, He threatened not but committed Himself to Him that judgeth righteously. (1 Pet. ii:23). He was oppressed, and He was afflicted, yet He opened not His mouth; He was brought as a lamb to the slaughter, and as a sheep before his shearers is dumb, so He opened not His mouth. All the buffetings, shame, dishonours, griefs, pains and sorrows He patiently endured. Oh! the patience of Christ, who for the joy set before Him endured the cross, despising the shame!

And into this patience of Christ, our hearts are to be directed. It is to be the object of our contemplation and to be followed by us, who belong to Him. The patience of Christ must be manifested in our lives. For even hereunto were ye called, because Christ also suffered for us, leaving us an example, that ye should follow His steps. His humility, submissiveness, contentment, calmness, patience in endurance, in doing and suffering the will of God, must be reproduced in our lives. But how little we know of it. Impatience is the leading characteristic of the closing days of this present evil age. It is alas! but too prominently seen among God's people who are influenced by the present-day currents. How little true waiting on the Lord and for the Lord is practised! How much reaching out after the things which are but for a moment and which will soon perish! In consequence, there is but little enjoyment of that which is the glorious and eternal portion of the Saints of God. How great the haste and hurry of present-day life! How little quietness and contentment! In suffering and loss, murmurings, fault-finding and words of forced resignation are more frequently heard than joyful songs of praise. Unrest instead of rest, discontent instead of contentment, anxiety instead of simple trust, self-exaltation instead of self-abnegation, ambitiousness instead of lowliness of mind are found on all sides among those who name the name of Christ and who carry His Life in their hearts. And why? Your heart, dear reader, is so often out of touch with Christ. You lose sight of Him. His Spirit is grieved and in consequence, there is a failure and the impatience of the flesh. Return, oh my soul, unto thy rest! Direct, O Lord, our hearts into the Patience of Christ.

The Patience of Christ. He is still the patient Christ. Rejected by the world He has taken His place upon the Father's throne. There He waits until His enemies are made His footstool. Long ago, in our human reckoning, He entered there. Long ago the Father said to Him, "Ask of Me and I will give Thee the heathen for thine inheritance, and the uttermost part of the earth for Thy possession" (Ps. 2:8). Up to now, He has not yet asked the Father. When He asks it will mean judgment for this world. In infinite patience, He has waited and waited in the presence of God. And all this time He has carried on His work as the Priest and Advocate of His people who live on earth. With what tenderness and patience, He has dealt with all who lived in the past centuries. His mighty power kept them and now they are at home with Him. The same patience He manifests towards us. How often we have failed Him and walked in the flesh instead of walking in the Spirit. We came to Him and confessed and then we found Him so loving towards us. But ere long we failed again and in His loving patience, His arms were again around us. And thus, a hundred times. He changeth not. He is the same loving, patient Lord towards His own in Glory as He was on earth. "He shall not be discouraged," the prophet declared. Even so, His Patience knows no discouragement.

In all the dishonour done to His holy, worthy Name, He endures patiently. He is silent to all what is done by His enemies. May the Lord grant us His Patience. John said to himself, "I am your brother and companion in the tribulation and in the kingdom and patience of Jesus Christ" (Rev. 1:9). To that kingdom and Patience of Jesus Christ of which John speaks of belonging we belong. The martyrs belonged to it. Afflictions, persecutions and sufferings were their part. They are ours. In humility, in endurance, unflinching courage, in the patience of Christ, let us suffer from Him, share His reproach until His Glory is revealed.

9) **Self-Control**

Before His ministry was launched, Jesus spent time being tempted by the Devil in the wilderness. Although He was offered food, power, and many other things, Jesus controlled His desires and submitted them all to the will of the Father. Yes, He had desires for food and such, but He had a greater desire to obey the Lord and accomplish what He set out to do. Anger is an aspect of our lives that we must deal with. Ecclesiastes 7:9, 'Be not hasty in thy spirit to be angry: for anger resteth in the bosom of fools'. There are three things about anger that we must watch out for, they are as follows:

a)   Anger gives room to the devil in our life. Ephesians 4:26-27 "Be angry, and do not sin": do not let the sun go down on your wrath, 27 nor give place to the devil." Anger becomes a sin when we embrace it for too long enough. When is too long I hear you ask? I answer that question with another one. How long would you want to have a headache before getting rid of it? I think the answer should be obvious. If you entertain anger Satan (or more precisely, his demonic forces) will have a doorway into your life. If you give Satan a place to stay he is sure to leave a mess. Ask brother Cain about it.

Anger grieves the Holy Spirit. Ephesians 4:30-31 "And do not grieve the Holy Spirit of God, by whom you were sealed for the day of redemption, Let all bitterness, wrath, anger, clamour, and evil speaking be put away from you, with all malice." Anger is mentioned above as one of the things that grieve the Holy Spirit. Maybe you have never seen it in that way before. As you let these words touch your heart you will discover the roots of anger in your life being cut away. As you read these words, I pray that they may bring you light. Grieving the Holy Spirit means a lack of anointing in our life. It is one of the reasons why there is a lack of the gifts of the Holy Spirit among many Christians today.

Anger affects our physical body - adversely. Genesis 4:6 "And the Lord said to Cain, why are you angry? And why do you look sad and depressed and dejected?" (The Amplified Bible). Cain was sad. His physical body was depressed.

His health was affected by his anger. Today even medical science acknowledges that anger can cause high blood pressure, headaches, irrational judgements and much more. If anger is a problem, you must treat it as a problem immediately. Just like you would to a headache. Ask the Lord for help.

10) **Humble**

Jesus had every opportunity and right to demand praise and accolades for His miracles and teachings, but He never did! Even when the crowds sought to make Him king, He rushed away from their grasp. He did not want to become a sideshow performance that people could enjoy. Rather, He wanted to seek and save the lost and offer forgiveness for sinful people. Yes, He could have travelled around in order to show off His powers in other towns, but He chose not to. Ten things that the bible says about humility:

1) Philippians 2: 3-11: Do nothing from rivalry or conceit but in humility count others more significant than yourselves. Let each of you look not only to his own interests but also to the interests of others. Have this mind among yourselves, which is yours in Christ Jesus, who, though he was in the form of God, did not count equality with God a thing to be grasped, but made himself nothing, taking the form of a servant, being born in the likeness of men...

2) James 4:6: But he gives more grace. Therefore, it says, "God opposes the proud, but gives grace to the humble."

3) Luke 14: 11: For everyone who exalts himself will be humbled, and he who humbles himself will be exalted.

4) Proverbs 22:4: The reward for humility and fear of the Lord is riches and honour and life.

5) 1 Peter 5:6: Humble yourselves, therefore, under the mighty hand of God so that at the proper time he may exalt you...

6) Romans 12:3: For by the grace given to me I say to everyone among you not to think of himself more highly than he ought to think, but to think with sober judgment, each according to the measure of faith that God has assigned.

7) Colossians 3:12: Put on then, as God's chosen ones, holy and beloved, compassionate hearts, kindness, humility, meekness, and patience.

8) Proverbs 11:12: When pride comes, then comes disgrace, but with the humble is wisdom.

9) 1 Peter 5:5: Likewise, you who are younger, be subject to the elders. Clothe yourselves, all of you, with humility toward one another, for "God opposes the proud but gives grace to the humble."

9:23: Thus says the Lord: "Let not the wise man boast in his wisdom, let not the mighty man boast in his might, let not the rich man boast in his riches,

Brethren you feel it is difficult to exhibit the Christ-like behaviour and we need to understand we need the grace of God to attain this level in our Christian life, Christlike attributes are gifts from God. They come as you use your agency righteously. Ask your Heavenly Father to bless you with these attributes; you cannot develop them without His help. With a desire to please God, recognize your weaknesses and be willing and anxious to improve.

Chapter 4

Key of David Upon your shoulder

The Key of David is a term found in Revelation and Isaiah. A key indicates control or authority; therefore, having the Key of David would give one control of David's domain, i.e., Jerusalem, the City of David, and the kingdom of Israel. The fact that, in Revelation 3:7, Jesus holds this key shows that He is the fulfilment of the Davidic Covenant, the ruler of the New Jerusalem, and the Lord of the kingdom of heaven. However, the passage in Revelation has been used inappropriately by a few cults that ultimately descend from the Christian Identity Movement via Armstrongism.

The Key of David is most directly referenced in Revelation 3:7, "To the angel of the church in Philadelphia write: These are the words of him who is holy and true, who holds the key of David." The Old Testament reference is Isaiah 22:22. There, the prophet tells the palace secretary Shebna that he will be replaced by Eliakim, for God "will place on his shoulder the key to the house of David" (Isaiah 22:22). The one who holds the keys has the authority. Thus, the "key of David" implies control of David's domain, which was promised to the Messiah in both the Old and New Testaments (Isaiah 9:7; Luke 1:32).

Paul told Timothy to avoid "myths and endless genealogies. These promote controversies rather than God's work—which is by faith" (1 Timothy 1:4). There is no "special knowledge" beyond the gospel itself that will aid salvation. Any claim beyond faith in the work of Jesus tears out the heart of the good news: that the just will live by faith (Romans 1:17). There is no great vision, special knowledge, or Jewish lineage needed, only faith in Christ.

This could also mean Dominion, which is the demonstration of power against every power of darkness, prophet Isaiah in chapter 22 verse 22 gave an account of the key of David upon the shoulder of the coming messiah, our argument would definitely spring up, what's our concern with this key? , as a child of God, we could lay claims on our inheritance as heir, heir of God and joint-heir with Christ(Rom 8:17). We need to be conscious of this and the only way we can have the keys upon our shoulder is to ensure we follow all that we have discussed in chapter three of this book, make holiness our lifestyle and above all exercise faith like a mustard seed.

John 14:12-13, 'Verily, verily, I say unto you, He that believeth on me, the works that I do shall he do also; and greater works than these shall he do; because I go unto my Father. And whatsoever ye shall ask in my name, that will I do, that the Father may be glorified in the Son.

During the Apostolic age, miracles that Jesus had done during his earthly ministry was replicated by his disciples, Peter in Acts 3:6, at the beautiful gates came in contact of a crippled beggar and he looked towards his direction which indicates that he wanted alms and the servant of

God declared, '….Silver and gold have me none; but such as I have to give I thee: In the name of Jesus Christ of Nazareth rise up and walk.' The statement received a seal from heaven and was accompanied with power and suddenly the ankle, joints of the crippled received some strength and he began to limp and the miracle was fully executed and the man that was once crippled started to walk.

What of the incidence in Acts 9:40, Peter raised the dead, her name is Dorcas a widow full of good works, there was confusion in the land of Joppa, fortunately, peter was around the corner and he was informed and he knelt down and prayed and said Tabita arise, she opened her eyes and saw peter and she got up.

These miracles took place after the ascension of our Lord Jesus Christ, today it is very possible to have experiences like this. There must be faith not only on the part of the one who works it but even more so on the part of the one who receives the miracle. For it may sometimes happen that the one through whom the miracle is accomplished, has only poor faith, but the one receiving it has the faith to be healed, and thus God grants it.

The Keys of David is released upon our shoulder, the question is whether we are in procession of the spiritual currency called faith, this will always make a remarkable difference in our lives and we must begin to see ourselves in the light that God can use us in diverse ways to dispel darkness from people's lives and the Lord will take us to this level in Jesus name.

Holiness is another factor that we must not joke with, let's ensure we live up to expectation in this light, many children of God swim in sin and engage in prayer, these prayers cannot be answered until we are ready to make amendments, without holiness no one will see God(Heb 12:14).

Can you imagine how the world would look like, let us look at statistics, A comprehensive demographic study of more than 200 countries finds that there are 2.18 billion Christians of all ages around the world, representing nearly a third of the estimated 2010 global population of 6.9 billion? Christians are also geographically widespread – so far-flung, in fact, that no single continent or region can indisputably claim to be the centre of global Christianity.

Imagine our population and let's assume the adult is about 1.5 billion, if these numbers are Christ-like in behaviour this indicates that there will be light all over the world, we can be seen as taking our rightful position in the society, we don't need to struggle over any issue most things troubling us will be settled on our knees. There is no need to fight, Agreement prayer and all will be well.

But unfortunately, despite these numbers we are still struggling, it's not because the Pentecostals are few, but we have not taken authority.

I want us to look at this article, 'Fifteen Reasons Our Churches Are Less Evangelistic Today' published on FEBRUARY 23, 2015 by THOM S. RAINER, founder and CEO of Church Answers, an online community and resource for church leaders. The article is as follows: almost any metric, the churches in our nation are much less evangelistic today than they were in the recent past. In my own denomination, we are reaching non-Christians only half as effectively as we were 50 years ago (we measure membership to annual baptisms). The trend is disturbing.

We certainly see the pattern in the early church where "every day the Lord added to them those who were being saved" (Acts 2:47). In too many of our churches today, the congregations are reaching no one for Christ in the course of an entire year.

The Poll

I conducted an unscientific Twitter poll recently to see what church leaders and church members thought of this trend, My specific question was: "Why do you think many churches aren't as evangelistic as they once were?" The responses arrived quickly and in great numbers, both in public tweets and indirect messages to me. Indeed, I was still receiving responses four days after I sent my Twitter question.

The Results

The response was highly informative for me. Here are the top fifteen responses listed in order of frequency:

Christians have no sense of urgency to reach lost people.

Many Christians and church members do not befriend and spend time with lost persons. Many Christians and church members are lazy and apathetic.

We are more known for what we are against than what we are for.

Our churches have an ineffective evangelistic strategy of "you come" rather than "we go." Many church members think that evangelism is the role of the pastor and the paid staff. Church membership today is more about getting my needs met rather than reaching the lost.

Church members are in a retreat mode as culture becomes more worldly and unbiblical. Many church members don't really believe that Christ is the only way of salvation. Our churches are no longer houses of prayer equipped to reach the lost. Churches have lost their focus on making disciples who will thus be equipped and motivated to reach the lost.

Christians do not want to share the truth of the gospel for fear they will offend others. Political correctness is too commonplace even among Christians.

Most churches have unregenerate members who have not received Christ themselves. Some churches have theological systems that do not encourage evangelism.

Our churches have too many activities; they are too busy to do the things that really matter.

So What Is the Solution?

I received hundreds of responses to this poll. There is obviously widespread concern about the lack of evangelism in our churches and among Christians.

Though we might claim that that the above example is only applicable to church in foreign lands and I have experienced this in the local church I once pastor, the Deaconess that we appointed as the coordinator of evangelism, she stormed my office and told me that the assignment I gave her that she cannot do it, I encouraged her and told her to continue, she was frustrated.

The workforce is lukewarm and not ready to go an extra mile for Jesus, on the day of evangelism you can only see only 3 workers, this shows that it is not seen as being important, the General overseer, Pastor E.A. Adeboye always talk about the need to evangelize and still they refuse to comply. I recalled that God spoke to me at Jos during one of the conferences and I shared it with the ministers, the Lord told me to print convert cards that would be used for evangelism, each worker should be given a card and it must be updated with details of their converts and the entire workforce refused. Each time I ask of their converts they refuse to speak, it's an indication that they don't engage in personal evangelism. All hope is not lost as we need to continue encouraging the workforce, though activities might be so much that's what we need to build our spirit man.

Most Churches should organize outreaches that will ensure that the soul is won, Church planting is an example, such a programme is a springboard for evangelism. We must not give up but continue to strive in this direction and the Lord will help us in Jesus name.

Brethren we can emulate the Christ-like behaviours, this will make us relevant as Christians and ensure we make positive contributions to our society, can you imagine how our lights will shine in our nation. We must deal with our inadequacies and get focused, let us not be entangled with the things of the world, ensure we make holiness our standard and remain steadfast in God's business.

www.ingramcontent.com/pod-product-compliance
Lightning Source LLC
Chambersburg PA
CBHW032036040426
42449CB00007B/903